Finding Y PLACE in Life and Ministry

Combining Spiritual Gifts with 4 (DISC)

Personality Types, Abilities, Passions, and

Experiences of Life

Finding Your Place In Ministry

Table of Contents

P
L
A
C
E

Personality Discovery Section

Learning Spiritual Gifts Section

Abilities Awareness Section

Connecting Passion with Ministry Section

Experiences of Life Section

Finding Your PLACE Profile

PLACE

Finding Your Place In Ministry

Dear Participant,

Why is it important to help people find their PLACE?

Today, more than any other time in history, people have more choices as to how to give their time. They find themselves asking, "Where do I fit in?" "Why am I here?" "What can I do to make a lasting difference in my life and the lives of others?"

This assessment tool is part of a self-discovery process called PLACE. PLACE begins with a comprehensive exploration of the unique gifts and talents of each individual. The Bible-based curriculum can bring about radical transformations by helping people discover their personality, spiritual gifts, abilities, life passions and experiences, understand them, and put them to work.

> **P** – **Personality Discovery**
> **L** – **Learning Spiritual Gifts**
> **A** – **Abilities Awareness**
> **C** – **Connecting Passion with Ministry**
> **E** – **Experiences of Life**

God created each of us for a purpose. *"For we are God's workmanship created in Christ Jesus to do good works, which God prepared in advance for us to do"* (Ephesians 2:10). Part of His purpose for us is to edify the church and to serve in its ministries. *"...to prepare God's people for works of service, so that the Body of Christ may be built up"* (Ephesians 4:12). The PLACE process can help you discover how God has uniquely designed you, and it will help you realize His purpose for your life.

PLACE is a valuable tool in assisting churches and church staff members as they help people in their journey with God and each other. The tool that follows will give you a great understanding of your unique God-given design. If you would like to understand and experience the teaching that goes along with the tool, you may order the Finding Your PLACE in Ministry Personal Discovery Set, attend a workshop hosted by PLACE Ministries and a local church, or help introduce the PLACE process in your church. To find out more about the latest resources for ministry, please contact us. Call toll free 1-877-463-2863 or visit www.placeministries.org

Serving Him Together,

Jay McSwain

Introduction

Every Christian is on a journey that begins at the point of salvation. Along the way, it is important to discover your PLACE in the Body of Christ. You have a unique combination of Personality, Spiritual Gifts, Abilities, Passion, and Experiences that God designed to create your unique role in the work of His kingdom. *"...to prepare God's people for works of service, so that the Body of Christ may be built up"* (Ephesians 4:12).

God created each of us for a purpose. PLACE can help you discover your unique purpose and how He has equipped you to fulfill it in the Body of Christ, the Church. Completing this process will help you connect your passion and gifts in life to ministry within your church and it will help you discover a fulfilled Christian life through serving the Lord. Just as Jesus said, Christians find their life as they give it away. *"For whoever wants to save his life will lose it, but whoever loses his life for me will find it"* (Matthew 16:25).

Objective

In completing this tool, you will discover new insights about yourself and the way God has knit you together. This will enable you to experience the joy of Christian living by understanding your purpose here on earth.

You will discover a way to think about your Personality and how it interacts with your Spiritual Gift(s), your God-given Abilities, your Passions and your Life Experiences.

Your unique combination of Personality, Spiritual Gift(s), Abilities, Passion and Experiences can only be offered to the Body of Christ by you. This complete offering of everything we are is what the Apostle Paul spoke about in Romans 12:1, *"Therefore, I urge you, brothers, in view of God's mercy, to offer your bodies as living sacrifices, holy and pleasing to God - this is your spiritual act of worship."* In turn, a sense of confidence and direction by God's leading will help equip and empower you to find a PLACE of ministry. This experience will not only be pleasing to God, but will allow you to experience the joy of Christian living.

Benefits

▶ Gain the ability to evaluate ministry opportunities (Proverbs 22:6).

▶ Gain confidence in ministry situations (Romans 12:3).

▶ Gain insight into your unique design and purpose (Ephesians 2:10).

▶ Mature in your Christian walk (Ephesians 4:13).

▶ God will receive praise (1 Peter 4:11).

How Do I Understand My Personality Profile?

A personality profile is a way of categorizing people with similar characteristics into groups. These characteristics cause individuals to think and act in certain ways. An individual's profile is compiled by reviewing past beliefs, values, attitudes, actions, and behaviors. Looking at an individual's past thinking and behavior generally indicates that an individual will behave in similar patterns (ways) in the future.

For centuries people have studied personality and its impact on behavior. The first person credited with classifying personality types was Hippocrates, around 370 B.C. He categorized four personality temperaments according to bodily fluids. He called them choleric, melancholy, phlegmatic, and sanguine. His theory of bodily fluids determining behavior has been discredited, but the terminology has remained in classifying personality. During the 1900s, dozens of names have been used to describe the four basic personality types that Hippocrates developed hundreds of years ago.

In the 1920s and 30s, William Marston, a professor at Columbia University, developed the "DISC" model of human behavior to describe personality types. This model, like Hippocrates', was built around four personality types. There have been many adaptations of the "DISC" model since Marston's original work. What is presented in this assessment booklet is a simplified version of the original "DISC" model.

Everyone will have some characteristics from all four categories, but generally one or two categories will emerge as primary and secondary within a profile. There are no good or bad personality profiles. It is how we use our personality that makes it positive or negative. There are strengths and growth areas within each blend of the personality profiles. By understanding ourselves, we can maximize our strengths and minimize our weaknesses. Also, we will be able to understand others better and improve our relationship with all kinds of people.

KEY THOUGHTS: Personality Assessments do not account for the Holy Spirit living in and controlling a Christian's life. Also, they do no allow for emotional maturity, and skills that develop through training, and/or life experiences which all combine to teach us how to behave in situations.

Personality Assessment

INSTRUCTIONS: Every person is unique because of the Personality they have. This assessment can help guide you in the process of identifying your Personality. Read each of the following sets of responses to the numbered statements. Circle the one that most often describes you. When more than one applies, circle the one that would best describe you in your home, church, school, or work environment.

Example:

1. When it comes to thinking...
(A.) My keen mind knows what decisive actions to take.
B. I'm never overloaded, and I doubt there's such a thing as too much!
C. I know how to take someone else's idea and come up with concrete ways to put it to use.
D. I always search all possibilities in order to get to the bottom of things.

Once you have chosen your best response to each question, please follow the instructions on the scoring sheet at the end of the assessment.

1. When it comes to working on tasks...
A. I know I need your help, but I prefer to operate independently.
B. I love coming up with the ideas, but I prefer not to have to make it happen.
C. I know I'm idealistic and theoretical. My perfectionism may drive you nuts or make you glad I'm on the team.
D. My goal is to be as fair and inoffensive to others as possible.

2. The phrase I might repeat most often is...
A. "I'll do it myself."
B. "Why can't everyone get involved?"
C. "If it's worth doing, it's worth doing right."
D. "The more the merrier."

3. My favorite verse from Proverbs could be...
A. 17:22: *"Being cheerful keeps you healthy."*
B. 27:12: *"A sensible man watches for problems ahead and prepares to meet them..."*
C. 15:4: *"Gentle words cause life and health..."*
D. 11:14: *"Without wise leadership, a nation is in trouble..."*

4. It makes my day...
A. To know that I kept my cool when others were losing theirs.
B. To win. I just love beating the competition.
C. To make someone laugh, or to have someone appreciate my story .
D. To have everything in perfect order.

5. I absolutely hate...
A. Not being able to effect changes.
B. Feeling like I need to be "up" all the time.
C. Being pushed.
D. Being alone or not being able to talk.

6. In my overall attitude, I am more...
A. Unemotional and action-oriented than most.
B. Introverted and reflective than most.
C. Low-key and accepting than most.
D. Extroverted and optimistic than most.

7. Of course...
A. They must be upset with me – they passed me at church this morning and didn't even speak!
B. I would never get impatient if others would just do what I told them to do when I told them to do it!
C. I am excited. This is just how excited looks on me.
D. It's not a lie! Well, maybe just a teeny bit of an exaggeration!

8. When it comes to working on tasks...
A. I create lots of energy and excitement, even on the boring tasks.
B. I tend to know the best way to accomplish things and don't hesitate in to tell others how to do it.
C. I often get so bogged down in the details that I can get frustrated and indifferent about the project.
D. I usually sense how to do things, but am hesitant about sharing my ideas.

9. My fantasy job would be...
A. Any job where I'm president or CEO.
B. Renting myself out as the "perfect party guest."
C. A mediator or counselor.
D. One that requires bringing organization and structure to a group.

10. Two weaknesses I have are...
A. Lack of follow-through and over-committing.
B. Being moody and pessimistic.
C. Being overbearing and pushy.
D. Lack of organization and discipline.

Personality Assessment

continued

11. At work...
- A. I often set the standards too high for myself and others.
- B. I'm easily distracted, and find it difficult to prioritize.
- C. I often lack motivation and find it difficult to set goals.
- D. I tend to be a workaholic, and get bored easily with details.

12. A hallmark I'm known for is my...
- A. Inability to accept change quickly.
- B. Adventurous spirit and willingness to take more risks than the average person.
- C. Deep thinking and cautiousness before making a decision.
- D. Animation and storytelling.

13. One thing you should know about me is...
- A. I'm warm, engaging, and fun to be around.
- B. At times I can be too forceful in trying to get something done.
- C. If I tell you I will do something, you can rest assured I'll do it!
- D. As much as I love making new friends, I often need the other person to make the first move.

14. If you watch me in a crowded situation, you'll probably see me standing
- A. Wherever I'm told to stand.
- B. Alone, or moving the crowd over to where I am.
- C. On the fringes, just outside of the action.
- D. In the center of the crowd.

15. As a friend...
- A. I'm usually popular, but might dominate conversations.
- B. I have many casual relationships, and might tend to use people.
- C. I'm fairly loyal, and may seem insecure socially.
- D. I have deep relationships and struggle making new friends.

16. As far as my leadership of people...
- A. I enjoy being part of a team and making sure no one gets their feelings hurt.
- B. I prefer to loosen things up on the team – help people relax and have a good time.
- C. I thrive in leadership roles and am very independent and self-confident.
- D. I make a better follower than a leader, and actually prefer it that way.

17. The most common phrase I hear about myself is...
- A. "He/She is always thinking and planning."
- B. "He/She is just a blast to be around."
- C. "He/She is so patient and calm."
- D. "Don't worry, he/she will handle everything."

18. I really thrive on...
- A. Creating fun and excitement for others.
- B. Taking special care with the details and logistics.
- C. Leading others to a mutual goal.
- D. Harmony and absence of conflict.

19. My family, friends, and co-workers would likely describe me as being...
- A. Persuasive about things I believe in.
- B. Playful and spontaneous.
- C. Non-confrontational about issues.
- D. Persistent when I am sure about something.

20. People admire me most for...
- A. My warmth, enthusiasm, humor, and people skills.
- B. My deep concern and compassion, and for being cautious and economical.
- C. My staying calm, cool, and collected, and being happy and well-balanced.
- D. My strong-willed leadership, decisiveness, and being goal-oriented.

21. People probably like this about the way I communicate with them...
- A. I am direct and don't mind speaking the truth.
- B. I can listen well and give good counsel.
- C. I express my thoughts and opinions in a precise and detailed way.
- D. They love my stories, and when I am in a positive mood it gives them a lift.

22. If someone tells me my idea can't be done...
- A. I just can't wait to prove them wrong, and I proceed with even more determination.
- B. I get discouraged and worry about all of the time I've wasted in planning.
- C. I'm usually glad, because it sounded like too much work anyway.
- D. I just thank them profusely and cheerfully quit.

23. When someone offends me, the first thought that might run through my head would be...
- A. I'm sure they didn't mean to do that to me ...
- B. Oh, it doesn't matter... really!
- C. They're not going to get away with that!
- D. Why do they keep doing that to me?

24. My philosophy about forgiveness is...
- A. "So ... what's there to forgive anyway?"
- B. "That was unforgivable..."
- C. "An eye for an eye."
- D. "Whatever ... don't worry about it."

Personality Profile Scoring and Graph

INSTRUCTIONS:

On the Personality Chart below, circle the letter you chose from the appropriate numbered question on the Personality Assessment. Add up the columns by counting how many times you circled a letter in that specific column. Transfer your totals to the graph below.

QUESTION	D	I	S	C
1	A	B	D	C
2	A	D	B	C
3	D	A	C	B
4	B	C	A	D
5	A	D	C	B
6	A	D	C	B
7	B	D	C	A
8	B	A	D	C
9	A	B	C	D
10	C	A	D	B
11	D	B	C	A
12	B	D	A	C
13	B	A	D	C
14	B	D	A	C
15	B	A	D	C
16	C	B	A	D
17	D	B	C	A
18	C	A	D	B
19	A	B	C	D
20	D	A	C	B
21	A	D	B	C
22	A	D	C	B
23	C	A	B	D
24	C	A	D	B
Totals				

INSTRUCTIONS:

Plot the totals from the Personality Chart to the Scoring Graph below. Once you have plotted all areas, connect the dots. If you score above the midpoint you will most likely demonstrate a higher level of affinity with the descriptions of that personality type than those scores below midpoint. Also, you will display a higher level of intensity with regards to that type of personality.

Transfer your personality blend to the Finding Your PLACE profile at the back of the book.

Personality Scoring Graph

D	I	S	C

```
24 ─
20 ─
16 ─
12 ─
 8 ─
 4 ─
 0 ─
```

What does it mean to be a...?

▷ Personality (Choleric)
Driven

- adventuresome
- aggressive
- arrogant
- authoritative
- blunt
- bold
- bossy
- brash
- career-driven
- confident
- controlling
- crafty
- decisive
- determined
- disciplined
- doer
- dominates a group
- domineering
- driven
- effective
- emphatic
- fast
- firm
- focused
- hard
- harsh
- hostile
- hot-tempered
- impatient
- impetuous
- impulsive
- initiating
- insensitive
- intense
- intuitive
- manipulative
- opportunist
- optimistic
- outgoing
- over-bearing
- persuasive
- practical
- productive
- quick
- restless
- self-confident
- self-disciplined
- self-sufficient
- single-minded
- short-tempered
- strong-willed
- task-oriented
- temperamental
- tenacious
- thick-skinned
- bull-headed
- unaffectionate
- unemotional

▷ Personality (Sanguine)
Inspiring

- bubbly
- carefree
- changeable
- charismatic
- charming
- childlike
- compassionate
- compromising
- conversation has a contagious quality that induces similar mood in hearers
- curious
- disorganized
- easily distracted
- easygoing
- emotional
- enjoys life
- enthusiastic
- exaggerates
- expressive
- extroverted
- eye for nature and art
- friendly
- impractical
- impulsive
- influencing
- insecure (masked by apparent self-confidence)
- insensitive
- inspiring
- lacks coherence in life because too "now" focused and too open to impressions
- lively
- loves being in the limelight
- natural magnetic grace
- optimistic
- outgoing
- people-centered
- persuasive
- popular
- positive
- responsive
- restless
- self-indulgent
- spontaneous
- superficial
- talkative
- tender
- undependable meeting deadlines
- undisciplined
- warm
- weak-willed

▷ Personality (Melancholy)
Conscientious

- artistic
- calculating
- cheerless
- competent
- concise
- conscientious
- conservative
- consistent
- controlling
- correct
- creative
- critical
- dependable
- depressed
- depressing
- detailed
- dissatisfied
- dissects self
- efficient
- faithful
- feels unapproved
- follow rules
- hard to get along with
- idealistic
- impatient
- impossible to please
- impractical
- inflexible
- intolerant
- introverted
- intelligent
- investigative
- irritable
- knowledgeable
- loyal
- methodical
- moody
- negative
- opinionated
- organized
- overly self-critical
- perfectionist
- pessimistic
- precise
- proud
- quality centered
- reserved
- revengeful
- rigid
- sacrificial
- self-centered
- contemplation leads to paralysis
- self-examining
- self-sacrificing
- self-torturous
- sensitive
- structured
- suspicious
- task-oriented
- theoretical
- thin-skinned
- traditional
- uncompromising
- unemotional
- not talkative
- values quality of life

▷ Personality (Phlegmatic)
Steady

- avoids risk
- calm
- cautious
- compromising
- consistent
- cool-headed
- cooperative
- dependable
- desires security
- diplomatic
- easily influenced
- efficient
- encourager
- faithful
- fearful
- flexible
- follows rules
- free-spirited
- good-natured
- indecisive
- kind
- lacks confidence
- lacks drive
- loyal
- naive
- needs affirmation
- non-confrontational
- not brittle under stress
- not easily aroused or disturbed
- passive
- patient
- peaceful
- people-oriented
- persistent
- placid
- planner
- practical
- protective
- puts down and limits feelings
- reserved
- self-protective
- sensitive
- shy
- sincere
- slow to change
- specialist
- stable
- steady
- stubborn regarding change
- submissive
- sweet
- team-oriented
- thoughtful
- timid
- unambitious
- unassertive

10

What does God Say About My Personality...?

D personalities need to learn to listen and not always speak their own opinions.

James 1:19 ...*Everyone should be quick to listen, slow to speak...*

D personalities need to be aware of their tendency to be angry.

Proverbs 16:32 *Better a patient man than a warrior, a man who controls his temper than one who takes a city.*

D personalities need to learn that love, joy, peace, patience, kindness, goodness, faithfulness, gentleness, and self-control are not options for a Christian.

Galatians 5:22-23 *But the fruit of the Spirit is love, joy, peace, patience, kindness, goodness, faithfulness, gentleness, and self-control...*

D personalities need to forgive others.

Ephesians 4:32 *Be kind and compassionate to one another, forgiving each other, just as in Christ, God forgave you.*

D personalities must place their faith in God and not in their own self-sufficiency.

Mark 11:22 *'...Have faith in God,' Jesus answered.*

D personalities are generally successful because of their strong will and determination.

I Corinthians 9:24-27 ...*Run in such a way to get the prize...*

D personalities are aggressive and display leadership qualities.

Acts 17:4 *And some of them were persuaded and joined Paul...*

I personalities need to learn that there is a time to be still.

Psalm 46:10 ...*be still and know that I am God.*

I personalities need to learn to listen to others.

Proverbs 19:20 *Listen to counsel...*

I personalities need to recognize the need for structure and organization.

I Corinthians 14:40 *Let all things be done properly and in an orderly manner.*

I personalities need to learn to be sensitive to the feelings of others.

Colossians 1:12 ...*put on a heart of compassion, kindness, humility, gentleness and patience.*

I personalities must work to have discipline in their lives.

II Timothy 2:15 *Study to present yourself approved to God...*

I personalities are bold in sharing their faith.

Acts 4:20 ...*for we cannot stop speaking what we have seen and heard.*

I personalities look for opportunities to help others.

Galatians 6:10 ...*let us do good to all men.*

I personalities do not waver between God's call and immediate action once they understand it.

Mark 1:17-18 *'Follow Me',... And they immediately left...*

I personalities do not find it hard to obey God's command to assemble together.

Hebrews 10:25 ...*not forsaking our own assembling together...*

C personalities must recognize that much of the Christian life has to be lived by faith.

I Corinthians 12:12 ...*now I know in part...*

C personalities struggle with forgiving those who have wronged them.

Ephesians 4:32 ...*forgiving each other, just as God in Christ also has forgiven you.*

C personalities often allow their thinking to be negative and can allow this negative thinking to lead to depression.

Philippians 4:8 ...*whatever is true, whatever is honorable, whatever is right, whatever is pure, whatever is lovely, whatever is of good repute, if there is any excellence and if anything worthy of praise, let your mind dwell on these things.*

C personalities need to guard against using words to criticize others.

Proverbs 15:1 *A gentle answer turns away wrath, but a harsh word stirs up anger.*

C personalities do not struggle with being humble.

C personalities set the example when it comes to having things done properly and in order.

I Corinthians 14:40 *But let all things be done properly and in an orderly manner.*

C personalities strive to keep doctrine pure and unadulterated.

II Timothy 2:15 ...*handling accurately the word of truth to show thyself approved, rightly dividing the word.*

C personalities do not struggle with the command to correct wrongs when they are obvious.

II Timothy 4:2 ...*reprove, rebuke, exhort with great patience.*

S personalities use their soft, sensitive words to resolve conflict.

Proverbs 15:1 *A soft answer turns away wrath.*

S personalities stay loyal even when someone has failed them.

Proverbs 17:17 *A friend loves at all times...*

S personalities are able to bring peace to unsettled situations by their words and attitude.

Ephesians 1:2 *Grace to you and peace from God our Father and the Lord Jesus Christ.*

S personalities often lack confidence.

Exodus 4:1 *What if they will not believe me, or listen to what I say?*

S personalities must learn not everyone is sincere and truthful.

Ephesians 4:6 *Let no one deceive you with empty words...*

S personalities need to have confidence in the gifts God has given them.

Romans 12:3 ...*God has allotted to each a measure of faith.*

S personalities shy away from responsibilities that require exposure of wrong/harsh action.

Ephesians 4:11 ...*do not participate in the unfruitful deeds of darkness, but instead even expose them.*

How does my Personality affect my thinking?

D

→ *Tends to be Non-reflective, Reactive* ←

I

Tends to be Pragmatic, Practical, Realistic

Tends to be Romanticist, Imaginative, Idealist

D Personality (Choleric)

D's are known for their keen, quick minds. They use their sharp and highly intuitive perceptions of people and situations to "know" what needs to be done; they then focus themselves and others on the ideal kind of action that gets things done. As realists who are relatively practical, D's may only think deep and long enough to create a workable plan without much concern for underlying theory. Thus, their thinking can be crafty, driven, and purposeful, but also lack calm foresight, imagination, and sufficient planning. D's can be commonplace, humdrum, tiresome, dull, unimaginative, and boring in their thinking, and often find it hard to develop an inner life of meaningful reflection.

I Personality (Sanguine)

I's are awakened by and responsive to exciting and thrilling experiences. Their responses in life are direct and not particularly reflective or planned. I's tend to process their thoughts aloud and spontaneously, without organizing them in advance. Their thinking may come across to some other personalities as unclear, illogical, inconsistent, confused, and superficial. However, because they are always looking for "the new," they can often appreciate completely different approaches to dull things, and speak of the ordinary in very charming ways. I's need to learn the thinking arts of reflection and self-examination to combat their tendency to distraction, tangents, and shallowness.

C Personality (Melancholy)

C's have the most complex layered mental abilities of the four personalities. They want to get to the bottom of everything, and their thinking is deep, thorough, and reflective. C's will never be accused of being superficial or phony, but this has down sides. Their strong imagination tends to lead to romanticism, their analysis can lead to being judgmental, and their ordering can lead to perfectionism. Their tendency for idealism and perfectionism can lead to frequent disillusionment, which may fuel serious doubts and a desire to remove themselves even more from the real world through daydreaming. Still, C's are highly creative and sharply stimulating; their thoughts are well considered, expressed with originality, and they are highly conscientious.

S Personality (Phlegmatic)

S's tend to have a calm, clear intellect that is unclouded because of their generally unemotional nature. This tends to give them a good range of intellectual ability, although it may not be as deep or insightful as that of some other personalities. S's are often able to put to practical use the brilliant ideas of others. They have a no-nonsense, practical mind, which is less prone to "wishful thinking." However, they drift too easily into rationalism, and also tend to modify their ideals until they are workable.

C

→ *Tends to be Reflective, Contemplative* ←

S

△ **CAUTION**: In reviewing the following summaries regarding the DISC Personalities it will be important to remember several things:
• The Holy Spirit controlling each Personality type is not factored in these descriptions.   • Individuals will be a blend of more than one Personality type.
• Much of the language used in these comparisons is taken to an extreme.   • An individual will not relate to every descriptive word in these Personality descriptions.
• Personalities are not good or bad, it is what you do with them and Who is in control of them that makes the difference.

How does my Personality affect my emotions and how I control them?

D →Tends to be Hot, Expressive, and have Fluctuating Emotions← **I**

Tends to be Insensitive, Nonsentimental

D Personality (Choleric)

When it comes to emotions, D's are noted for being quick-tempered, abrupt, and hard. They are the most likely of the personalities to react in anger. Not only is their emotional nature unemotional, they have no use for sensitivity and can be unfeeling. This means they do not sympathize well with others' pain or grief. They may appear very thick-skinned, and do not comprehend what is tender, delicate, and fragile in life. It can be difficult to interest D's in religion, as they see it as mere emotionalism.

I Personality (Sanguine)

Intense but inconsistent feelings predominate in the world of I's. They are very sensitive and have a rich, broad-ranged emotional life. Their emotions are easily stirred by impressions from the outside world – either in constructive or destructive directions – and their typical overreactions often lead to "a mood." But emotions are fleeting, and I's frequently experience quick reversals of feeling. They may go from sulking to elation. This emotionality affects their involvement in causes, by which they are easily and intensely interested ...for the moment. In expressing their feelings, I's tend to be talkative, extreme, vivid, and emphatic.

C Personality (Melancholy)

Feelings predominate C's, giving them a rich, sensitive nature (often over-sensitive, easily crushed). Ironically, C's typically feel more than they can express. For instance, C's are not quick-tempered, but can erupt in pent-up anger. Sadly, they are pessimistic, moody, and preoccupied with their own emotional pain. C's constantly dissect themselves, and see little in their world that is encouraging. Impressions of self can dig and bury deeply and work actively in their imaginations, leading to depression – as when promises they break or errors they make may distress them for a long time or even a lifetime!

S Personality (Phlegmatic)

S's are frequently described as dependable, tranquil, and cool. They maintain their inner emotional balance and come across as easy-going and levelheaded in all situations. Because S's are clear-minded and levelheaded, they do not become restless or annoyed by imperfection. They are not caught off guard, not tense, and not into reform and change. They have the strength and presence of mind to assess risky situations calmly, consider the possibilities, and choose the best way out. But for all the potentially positive dimensions of those character qualities, on the downside, S's are also sometimes empty-hearted, dispassionate, and indifferent.

Tends to be Sensitive, Sentimental

C → Tends to be Dispassionate, Repressive, and Smoldering ← **S**

△ **CAUTION:** In reviewing the following summaries regarding the DISC personalities it will be important to remember several things:
- The Holy Spirit controlling each Personality type is not factored in these descriptions.
- Much of the language used in these comparisons is taken to an extreme.
- Personalities are not good or bad, it is what you do with them and Who is in control of them that makes the difference.
- Individuals will be a blend of more than one Personality type.
- An individual will not relate to every descriptive word in these Personality descriptions.

How does my Personality affect my will and my self-discipline?

D →Tends to have a Higher Level of Risk-Taking← **I**

Tends to have a Higher Level of Self-Discipline

Tends to have a Lower Level of Self-Discipline

D Personality (Choleric)

For D's, will is the controlling factor. Life consists of action and work as a show of their urge toward self-determination and a response to external factors. (D's also like making decisions for others.) They possess strong will power, a sharp mind, focus, and stamina which helps their actions be quick, bold, and decisive, though perhaps hasty and impulsive. D's are not dismayed by barriers or adversities, but see oppositions as challenges that spur them on in their adventures. They are risk-takers, avoiding the safe and everyday, and drawn to the hazardous and unknown. D's often are active, but unreflective; unyielding, but over the edge; persistent but practical; fiery but foolhardy.

I Personality (Sanguine)

When it comes to self-discipline, I's have good hearts, but undependable follow-through. Their will is not particularly stirred, and so their actions are unpredictable and inconsistent, even if they show initiative in new ideas or projects. I's may prove spontaneous and surprising, but are also shallow, forgetful, and distracted. They may even invent excuses for why they "could not" (actually, "did not") carry out their obligations. They may be the Personality most likely to enjoy life, but also to leave this world with a trail of unaccomplished goals. The bottom line: They have good intentions in their promising, but are unreliable in deciding, and weak-willed in persevering.

C Personality (Melancholy)

Making decisions and engaging in calculated risks are not strong points for C's, in part due to their passive nature. Also, their capacity for endless analysis of every possible angle and consequence paralyzes them. The more possible outcomes C's find, the more difficult it is for them to decide. They finally act only when they must, and then with ongoing doubts and small measures of boldness. C's are also relatively self-disciplined and know their limitations. They would rather commit to fewer and safer things, and finish what they undertake than make promises they know they can't keep. Though they are not risk-takers, C's are self-sacrificers and dependable servants.

S Personality (Phlegmatic)

Decision-making and self-discipline are problems for S's. They are often slow, sluggish, and easygoing. Because they don't like inconvenience, they are unwilling to exert themselves or be in a hurry. They do consider issues before acting, but still find it hard to overcome their inertia and tendency to procrastinate. Once S's get moving, they can lay out good plans, efficiently execute them, and prove themselves dependable in follow-through. More often, though, they are calm spectators who are not swayed by emotion. They take the easiest ways instead of being farsighted, and stagnate instead of persevere. S's can be so practical they compromise their standards when convenient.

C →Tends to have a Lower Level of Risk-Taking← **S**

△ **CAUTION**: In reviewing the following summaries regarding the DISC personalities it will be important to remember several things:
- The Holy Spirit controlling each Personality type is not factored in these descriptions.
- Much of the language used in these comparisons is taken to an extreme.
- Personalities are not good or bad, it is what you do with them and Who is in control of them that makes the difference.
- Individuals will be a blend of more than one Personality type.
- An individual will not relate to every descriptive word in these Personality descriptions.

How does my Personality affect how I relate to other people?

D →Tends to have More Friends and Shallower Friendships← **I**

Tends to Need People

Tends to be Loyal and Stick With People

D Personality (Choleric)

Relationships can be a problem for D's, who often act out their Personality in self-centered ways that show disrespect and lack of consideration for others. D's are seen as overly self-confident, proud, and haughty. Although they can be good leaders, they can also be domineering in relationships, lack patience with people, and not appreciate the abilities in others. D's often lack compassion for those who are suffering, whether physically, emotionally, or spiritually. They also use their good judgment of human nature to gain information for their own advantage. Because they see people as tools for their plans, they may be clever, manipulative, and show false concern to get their way. D's consider apologizing as perhaps the ultimate humiliation; thus, committing to apologizing consistently can help conquer their relational weaknesses.

I Personality (Sanguine)

Overall, I's have the ability to establish heartwarming relationships with a wide range of people. They are warm, cheerful, and extravagant in relating. They accept people as they are, and aren't bothered by whether people meet certain standards or not. An I's receptive spirit helps them adjust to others and be genuinely interested in hearing their concerns. They do not disturb others' happiness with skepticism, criticism, or ridicule, but instead enter into their feelings and thoughts. I's are tender, sympathetic, and comforting. They are unlikely to become calloused toward people, and will consistently rejoice with those who rejoice and weep with those who weep. However, they also function by "out of sight, out of mind." This makes them unreliable, and easily charmed. Fortunately, of the four personalities, I's can humble themselves and apologize the most easily.

S Personality (Phlegmatic)

S's exercise a stabilizing influence in relationships, even in the midst of disturbing circumstances. They are evenly balanced, calm, and seldom stirred up. They are neither quick-tempered nor in a fuss about "stuff." S's are good-natured, easy to get along with, pleasant, cheerful, comfortable, and witty. But they can be apathetic, blasé, not cordial or demonstrative, to the point of being indifferent about others. S's often study people but have little interest in them, except when their opportunist tendencies see something on which they can capitalize. Otherwise, they can be disinterested spectators who seem apathetic. Their presence has a softening, conciliating effect upon others, and their love of peace and harmony gives them a base for relating with many different kinds of people successfully, and even bringing a unifying presence to groups.

C Personality (Melancholy)

C's have significant problems in relating. They do not make many friends, but those they make, they keep by being faithful, loyal, and dependable. They consider promises a point of honor to keep. However, C's are hard to get along with or touch, and they are proud. Their sharp ability to analyze lets them see faults in others clearly, and they become critical and judgmental. But their self-centeredness focuses them on how things affect them, not how *they* affect others. So they cannot analyze their own faults. Their romantic search for the ideal leads them to be uncompromising, disappointed, and self-protective. C's are easily hurt, suspicious, distant, and not joyful. They may have a persecution complex. They tend to daydream and harbor grudges, which can increase to unbearable proportions. C's may be the most likely Personality to create disharmony, and to blame, whine, and complain.

S →Tends to have Fewer Friends and Deeper Friendships← **C**

 CAUTION: In reviewing the following summaries regarding the DISC personalities it will be important to remember several things:
- The Holy Spirit controlling each Personality type is not factored in these descriptions.
- Much of the language used in these comparisons is taken to an extreme.
- Personalities are not good or bad, it is what you do with them and Who is in control of them that makes the difference.
- Individuals will be a blend of more than one Personality type.
- An individual will not relate to every descriptive word in these Personality descriptions.

How does my Personality affect my leadership roles?

D → **Tends to Want an Environment of Control** ← **C**

Tends to Lead and be Active

D Personality (Choleric)

D's love to lead and will often volunteer to do so. Ironically, D's want an environment of freedom *and* of control so they can do what they want. Their action-orientation does not mean their plans are any better than those developed by other personalities, but their aggressive, firm, and consistent nature pushes their plans through. The leadership/authority style of D's tend to be energetic, impulsive, self-confident, reckless, forceful, crafty, achievement-minded, dictatorial, and bossy. D's bring goal-orientation and action to a group; they can also bring an opportunistic end justifies the means mentality, and a stubborn spirit.

C Personality (Melancholy)

Primarily passive, C's would rather be followers, not leaders. Still, they display helpful leadership qualities, such as their self-denial and service, uncompromising nature, and willingness to work behind the scenes. C's effectively analyze plans for their strengths and weaknesses. Unfortunately, this can make it appear they are against projects. But an ability to judge well does not necessarily mean one is judgmental. C's are prone to be negative, in part because they truly can anticipate upcoming and approaching flaws in plans and actions. They battle disappointment over outcomes that do not match promises. C's know their limitations and rarely take on more than they should/could do.

Tends to Submit and be Passive

I Personality (Sanguine)

Ironically, I's enjoy being free and unrestrained, while at the same time they are controlled and driven by external forces. I's embrace freedom, and are not governed by rules and regulations. They are easily molded by their environment. I's are also susceptible to "conning" themselves and others into following a path where the end justifies the means.

S Personality (Phlegmatic)

S's generally won't take leadership upon themselves. They are, however, quite capable when called into a leadership role. S's value freedom, yet, ironically, oppose change and can control situations by dragging their feet or even damaging a project when they don't really want to participate in it. When forced into the activities of others that turn out poorly, this fuels a deeper resistance to future activities. S's do not start projects. They are too much work for their laid-back disposition. S's are especially subject to compromising their ideals.

I → **Tends to Want an Environment of Freedom** ← **S**

⚠ **CAUTION**: In reviewing the following summaries regarding the DISC Personalities it will be important to remember several things:
- The Holy Spirit controlling each Personality type is not factored in these descriptions.
- Much of the language used in these comparisons is taken to an extreme.
- Personalities are not good or bad, it is what you do with them and Who is in control of them that makes the difference.
- Individuals will be a blend of more than one Personality type.
- An individual will not relate to every descriptive word in these Personality descriptions.

How does my Personality affect my communication style?

D ← **Tends to be More Talkative** → **I**

Tends to be Less People-Oriented

Tends to be More People-Oriented

D Personality (Choleric)

D's may be extroverted, but that does not mean they communicate clearly or kindly with people. D's are often known for finding it difficult to apologize or show approval, and often for communicating disapproval. They can speak in ways that are blunt and sarcastic, cutting, stinging, unaffectionate, and harsh. D's are so driven by their own goals that they tend not to focus on others or listen to what they are saying. They don't care if people disagree with them, they'll do what they want to anyway. Their communication is direct and to the point. Others generally know what D's think about a subject or another person. D's are extremely good at communicating goals and direction for themselves and others.

I Personality (Sanguine)

I's are sociable; words come easily to them. They process their thoughts aloud in a stream that does not include much thinking before they speak. Their style can be noisy, boasting and friendly, impressive, direct, and fascinating. They draw people in, but dominate discussions with topics of personal interest. Still, their conversation is contagious, and it creates similar moods in the listener. I's speak charmingly about everyday things, and are dramatic, colorful storytellers because of their emotional nature. I's are restless, making it hard to concentrate on listening to others. But they do apologize readily.

C Personality (Melancholy)

C's generally have opinions (and are often well-informed) about many topics and issues, but they generally withhold them from a conversation unless asked directly what they think. They are accurate and detailed, and tend to dislike exaggeration and ill-advised words. C's often are suspicious and depressing, which does not endear them to others in conversation. Others find it extremely easy to follow a C's directions because they are patient when communicating details. They do not communicate words they do not mean. What they say is what they mean. There are no hidden motives in their communication.

S Personality (Phlegmatic)

S's rate very different evaluations on their communication style. On the one hand, they are said to sometimes have an easygoing manner that makes it easy for them to listen to others, and that they can be quite counselor-oriented. On the other hand, they have been noted for their hesitation to become involved with others. They communicate in a calm and peaceful tone and do not generate lots of excitement for those listening. They bring harmony through their words and tend to use words that are not strongly positive or negative. They rarely communicate their disapproval of others. Even when they do, it may be difficult to detect.

C ← **Tends to be Less Talkative** → **S**

△ **CAUTION:** In reviewing the following summaries regarding the DISC personalities it will be important to remember several things:
- The Holy Spirit controlling each Personality type is not factored in these descriptions.
- Much of the language used in these comparisons is taken to an extreme.
- Personalities are not good or bad, it is what you do with them and Who is in control of them that makes the difference.
- Individuals will be a blend of more than one Personality type.
- An individual will not relate to every descriptive word in these Personality descriptions.

How does my Personality affect how I act when I'm offended?

D

More Present – to Future-Oriented

I

Tends to Dwell on Offenses, Be Bitter, Take Revenge

D Personality (Choleric)

D's are known for being revengeful. They do not easily forgive or forget an insult or an injury. Instead, they allow these to encourage them into future actions where they repay people for what they perceive as injustices or wrongs committed against them. D's tend to be bitter, wrathful, and angry, which, along with the other elements in their response to offenses, makes them ulcer-prone.

I Personality (Sanguine)

In general, I's forget the past easily and live in the present. Therefore, they tend to quickly forget offenses against them and move on.

C Personality (Melancholy)

C's are revengeful. In many ways, they live in the past, and find it difficult to forget any kind of insult or offense. Their unforgiving spirit serves to compound the impact of the offense and push it into the future; reflecting on the hurt drives it deeper as the slow-burner on their emotions makes them prone to boil with resentment inside. They carry grudges and become bitter and prejudiced against people because of unforgiveness.

S Personality (Phlegmatic)

S's wave off offenses as irrelevant, and so do not take offense as easily as other personalities. They live more in the present, not the past, and do not carry grudges when they have felt offended. They are peace loving, have a high boiling point, and seldom explode in anger. However, when they do explode it is in a cold and vengeful manner.

Tends to Forgive Offenses, Release, Move On

C

More Past- to Present-Oriented

S

⚠ **CAUTION**: In reviewing the following summaries regarding the DISC personalities it will be important to remember several things:
- The Holy Spirit controlling each Personality type is not factored in these descriptions.
- Much of the language used in these comparisons is taken to an extreme.
- Personalities are not good or bad, it is what you do with them and Who is in control of them that makes the difference.
- Individuals will be a blend of more than one Personality type.
- An individual will not relate to every descriptive word in these Personality descriptions.

How Do I Understand
My Spiritual Gifts Assessment?

When you become a Christian, the Holy Spirit gives you a Spiritual Gift or Gifts. This assessment will help guide you in the process of discovering your Spiritual Gift(s). This assessment will not tell you definitely if you do or do not have a certain Gift. For many, it will help confirm the Gift(s) they may believe they have, and for others it will begin the journey of discovering their Gifts. For everyone, it will be an illustration of the incredible love God has in giving His children Gifts to carry out their ministry here on earth.

You may score high in one area of the assessment because you have a passion for a particular area of ministry that correlates with a Spiritual Gift. For example, you may have a passion for evangelism, but you may not necessarily have the Gift of evangelism. Training and life experiences can cause a person to score high in a Gift. Our motives can also cause the assessment scores to be high or low for a particular Gift.

Keep in mind there are many roles that all Christians are commanded by God to carry out, even if we are not Gifted in the area. For example, we are all called to share our faith even if we do not possess the Gift of evangelism. God will always equip us to carry out each role that He expects us to fulfill.

In completing this assessment, the following principles will help you discover your Spiritual Gift(s):

- Believe you have a Spiritual Gift(s).
- Ask God to reveal your Spiritual Gift(s).
- Study the Scriptures relating to Spiritual Gifts.
- Explore possibilities by serving short-term in various ministries.
- Evaluate your effectiveness as you explore possibilities.
- Expect confirmation by others.
- Examine your feelings as you explore possibilities.
- Examine your motives for using a Gift.

If you have been a Christian for less than one year, it may be difficult for you to answer some of the questions because many are based on past experiences. Take heart, you do have a Gift(s). As God gives you ministry opportunities in which to serve, your Gift(s) will be revealed to you. Your Gifts do not change over time. Your experiences will change, however, which will often change the results of an assessment like the following one.

16 Spiritual Gifts Assessment

INSTRUCTIONS: Every person is given Spiritual Gift(s) at the time they accept Christ. This assessment can help guide you in the process of identifying your Spiritual Gift(s). Please follow these instructions:

Ask yourself how you feel about each one of the following statements. How true is each statement about you?

Respond with the numerical rating as follows:

5 – Almost Always true

4 – Often true

3 – Sometimes true

2 – Seldom true

1 – Almost Never true

Avoid, as much as possible, a 3 (Sometimes) choice. Don't hesitate choosing 5 (Almost Always) or 1 (Almost Never). Your desire to be humble or not exaggerate may cause you to choose more moderate responses. This may affect your results. Try to be as honest as possible.

Example:

1. I understand the truths of God's Word.

(Is this statement "Almost Always," "Often," "Sometimes," "Seldom" or "Almost Never" true about you? Try to choose the "5, 4, 2 or 1." Avoid choosing the 3 "Sometimes.")

Place your numerical rating choice in the appropriate blank before each statement on this and the next pages. Then, follow the instructions on the scoring sheet at the end of the assessment.

____ **1.** When I hear evangelistic messages, I pray for people who don't know Christ.

____ **2.** I am drawn to opportunities where I can give direction to others.

____ **3.** When others tell me their problems, I can deeply feel their hurt.

____ **4.** I am gifted at organizing tasks in a systematic manner.

____ **5.** When I see wrong, I feel compelled to speak.

____ **6.** I enjoy giving financial and material resources without the recipient knowing who gave.

____ **7.** I am able to clearly and effectively explain truths within God's Word.

____ **8.** Believers who stray from the faith really concern me and I actively seek to bring them back.

____ **9.** For me, it's easy to trust God for the impossible.

____ **10.** I frequently find myself encouraging the troubled, comforting the distressed, and reassuring the wavering.

____ **11.** When someone asks me to do a job, I get excited even when the job isn't highly visible to others

____ **12.** Coming alongside individuals and supporting them in their ministries brings me great satisfaction.

____ **13.** When I discover Biblical truths, I make skillful and practical applications of them into my life situations.

____ **14.** I perceive and understand the truths of God's Word.

____ **15.** I am happier entertaining guests at church or in my home than when I am alone.

____ **16.** People tell me that I can see through phonies before others do.

____ **17.** I enjoy building relationships and spending time with non-Christians.

____ **18.** Group problems are more interesting to me than individual problems.

____ **19.** I tend to have compassion for those who are rejected by others.

____ **20.** I plan details of an event thoroughly, analytically, and well in advance of the deadline.

____ **21.** When individuals or groups depart from God's Word, I can sense the coming danger and am willing to voice a warning.

____ **22.** I would sacrifice materially in order for more of my resources to go to Christian causes.

____ **23.** It irritates me when a speaker uses a Bible verse out of context.

____ **24.** I enjoy relating to a specific group of believers over an extended period of time.

____ **25.** I am able to envision God's leading in unlikely circumstances, and work to accomplish what I believe is His will.

____ **26.** I like to suggest practical steps for people to overcome challenges, but focus on investing myself in those who take action on my advice.

____ **27.** I enjoy doing tasks that others tend to have no desire to do.

____ **28.** I volunteer for tasks that appear routine, but which enable others to be more effective in leading.

____ **29.** I am able to know, understand, and apply God's Word in communicating to others.

____ **30.** I enjoy studying the Bible, investigating the full meaning of a text, and exploring the context of individual words and phrases.

____ **31.** I have been told that I make strangers feel welcome around me in my home, at church, and/or in other settings.

____ **32.** When I read a religious book, I'm able to detect outright errors from the truth.

____ **33.** Telling others how I came to accept Christ is a regular part of my lifestyle.

____ **34.** God uses me to motivate others to see His vision for the group.

____ **35.** People who are hurting and in need attract my attention and time.

____ **36.** "Multi-tasking," or doing multiple jobs simultaneously, is something I do efficiently.

____ **37.** I will expose sin even when it is unpopular or no one agrees with my conviction.

____ **38.** For me, it's easy to give to God's work beyond the 10% tithe.

____ **39.** People compliment me on making difficult subjects easy to understand.

____ **40.** Responsibilities where I can assume the spiritual oversight of a group of people draw my time and attention.

____ **41.** I commit difficult obstacles to God in prayer and am not anxious about His answering those prayers.

____ **42.** My preferred ways to teach and be taught are through practical application and Biblical illustrations.

____ **43.** In a group setting, I quickly assess needs and don't hesitate to help meet those needs.

____ **44.** If I know others are being helped, I enjoy doing things behind the scenes.

____ **45.** I grasp truths from God's Word, organize them, and relate them to the practical needs and problems of life.

____ **46.** When a speaker gives details of Biblical words, studies, and archeology, I find myself listening intently.

____ **47.** I believe a Christian's home should be a safe place for those in need.

____ **48.** I sense when the atmosphere in a worship service is mere emotion, versus emotion directed by the Holy Spirit.

____ **49.** I can clearly, concisely, and effectively communicate the gospel to non-Christians.

____ **50.** I have an ability to inspire and encourage others to perform at a high level.

____ **51.** I do not try to provide steps to solve people's problems; I just want to be available to them in their time of need.

____ **52.** I can organize and direct toward specific goals and in an orderly manner.

____ **53.** People tell me that I am outspoken and opinionated, especially on doctrinal issues.

____ **54.** Public recognition for giving a financial gift is not something I enjoy.

____ **55.** I thoroughly research a subject before speaking about it.

____ **56.** I find myself working hard to help others grow spiritually.

____ **57.** I regularly attempt to motivate others to believe God in difficult or impossible situations.

____ **58.** I really relate to speakers who give practical steps for applying Christian principles.

_____ 59. To help out a ministry, I prefer doing task-oriented projects rather than working one-on-one with people.

_____ 60. It is my preference to serve ministries by working directly with people rather than in task-oriented projects.

_____ 61. In my daily experience, I regularly put Bible knowledge to work.

_____ 62. People tell me that I help them understand important facts from Scripture.

_____ 63. People compliment me for my recognition of guests at church and allowing others to stay at my home.

_____ 64. I can immediately spot cult teachings that mix some truth with many false teachings.

_____ 65. I believe most churches do not emphasize evangelism enough.

_____ 66. When it comes to goals, I can match people and resources to achieve success.

_____ 67. It's hard for me to say "no" to those who are hurting and in need.

_____ 68. The kind of volunteer opportunities I look for involve organizing the big picture into small, do-able parts.

_____ 69. I view many activities as black or white, right or wrong for Christians to participate in.

_____ 70. I prefer to give my financial resources, rather than my time, to the Lord's work.

_____ 71. I enjoy teaching others Biblical truths in order for them to apply these truths.

_____ 72. God has used me to bring Christians who stray away from Him back into a growing relationship with Him and His people.

_____ 73. Even in negative situations, I view myself as an optimist.

_____ 74. Getting people involved in ministry through positive motivation is something I do effectively.

_____ 75. I need to feel appreciated for my contribution to a ministry.

_____ 76. I'd rather work behind the scenes without public recognition.

_____ 77. Exercising spiritual insight into the right or wrong of complicated situations is something I do well.

_____ 78. I help others in studying their Bible by sharing my discoveries of how various details of individual words and phrases fit into the passage's main idea.

_____ 79. I consider it a privilege to entertain guests at church and/or home, and I desire to take care of such needs as food for them.

_____ 80. When others are being deceptive in their actions and motives, I am usually aware of it.

_____ 81. It excites me tremendously when someone comes to know Christ.

_____ 82. People often look to me for direction when there is no clearly established leader in the group.

_____ 83. Helping others is something I have a strong inner drive to do.

_____ 84. I strive to create harmony when I am in charge of planning an event.

_____ 85. Those who speak straightforwardly draw my attention and time.

_____ 86. I believe financial accountability is vital.

_____ 87. No matter what other commitments I have, I always make time to study the Bible.

_____ 88. When it comes to taking care of others' needs, I willingly sacrifice my own needs and desires.

_____ 89. I often scold other Christians for their lack of faith.

_____ 90. Those who need encouragement when they have encountered disappointment draw my time and attention.

_____ 91. When people obviously see a need and don't volunteer to help solve it, that makes me angry.

_____ 92. I find it rewarding to take on responsibilities for others so they are free to concentrate on other aspects of ministry.

_____ 93. I find it easy to draw insight from my own study of the Scriptures and from the studies of other Bible scholars.

_____ 94. People often seek me out for my understanding of Biblical passages of interest to them.

_____ 95. I would be one of the first to affirm the church that is offering lodging for groups that are passing through and need a place to stay for a night or two.

_____ 96. I quickly recognize inconsistencies in teaching that is filled with error and is not Biblical.

_____ 97. I'm really energized after sharing Christ with a non-Christian.

_____ 98. I like new challenges and get bored with maintaining projects.

____ **99.** I volunteer to work with the underprivileged and poor.

____ **100.** I can identify and remove unnecessary details when organizing people or projects.

____ **101.** I tend to be suspicious and critical of contemporary culture.

____ **102.** I do not have hidden motives or secret agendas when I give financially.

____ **103.** I lean more toward explaining Biblical truths than applying them.

____ **104.** Any time Christians are under my care and influence, I naturally guard them from false teaching.

____ **105.** When I strongly believe God wants to accomplish great things in a group, I am often the one who encourages people to step out in faith and not be cautious.

____ **106.** I see trials as opportunities from God for spiritual growth.

____ **107.** I do not feel comfortable leading or delegating tasks to be done within a ministry.

____ **108.** People recognize me for my willingness to assist others so they can become more effective in their ministries.

____ **109.** When it comes to leading people, I am gifted at knowing, understanding, and applying God's Word.

____ **110.** I take seriously God's command to "increase in knowledge," and find it easy to commit regular blocks of time to fulfill this command.

____ **111.** It is important for churches to provide lodging when there is a need.

____ **112.** Christians frequently affirm my ability to discern truth from lies and/or counterfeits.

Notes

Spiritual Gifts Scoring and Graph

INSTRUCTIONS:
Record the number you chose for each of the Spiritual Gifts Questions in the corresponding numbered box below. Once you have recorded the scores and added the total for each column, please chart the graph below by circling the total points for that specific Spiritual Gift. Once all the columns have been circled, please connect the dots beginning with the first column.

Transfer your spiritual gifts scores to the Finding Your PLACE profile at the back of this book.

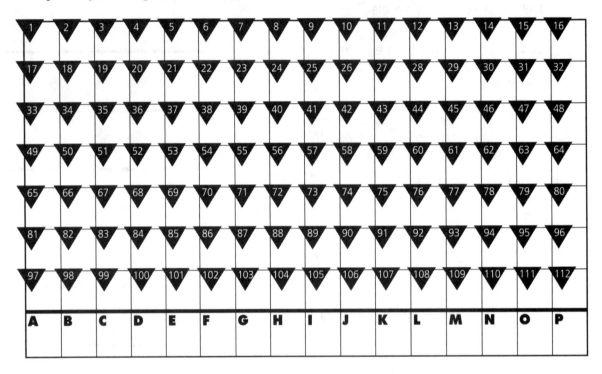

SPIRITUAL GIFTS GRAPH

A	B	C	D	E	F	G	H	I	J	K	L	M	N	O	P
35	35	35	35	35	35	35	35	35	35	35	35	35	35	35	35
34	34	34	34	34	34	34	34	34	34	34	34	34	34	34	34
33	33	33	33	33	33	33	33	33	33	33	33	33	33	33	33
32	32	32	32	32	32	32	32	32	32	32	32	32	32	32	32
31	31	31	31	31	31	31	31	31	31	31	31	31	31	31	31
30	30	30	30	30	30	30	30	30	30	30	30	30	30	30	30
29	29	29	29	29	29	29	29	29	29	29	29	29	29	29	29
28	28	28	28	28	28	28	28	28	28	28	28	28	28	28	28
27	27	27	27	27	27	27	27	27	27	27	27	27	27	27	27
26	26	26	26	26	26	26	26	26	26	26	26	26	26	26	26
25	25	25	25	25	25	25	25	25	25	25	25	25	25	25	25
24	24	24	24	24	24	24	24	24	24	24	24	24	24	24	24
23	23	23	23	23	23	23	23	23	23	23	23	23	23	23	23
22	22	22	22	22	22	22	22	22	22	22	22	22	22	22	22
21	21	21	21	21	21	21	21	21	21	21	21	21	21	21	21
20	20	20	20	20	20	20	20	20	20	20	20	20	20	20	20
19	19	19	19	19	19	19	19	19	19	19	19	19	19	19	19
18	18	18	18	18	18	18	18	18	18	18	18	18	18	18	18
17	17	17	17	17	17	17	17	17	17	17	17	17	17	17	17
16	16	16	16	16	16	16	16	16	16	16	16	16	16	16	16
15	15	15	15	15	15	15	15	15	15	15	15	15	15	15	15
14	14	14	14	14	14	14	14	14	14	14	14	14	14	14	14
13	13	13	13	13	13	13	13	13	13	13	13	13	13	13	13
12	12	12	12	12	12	12	12	12	12	12	12	12	12	12	12
11	11	11	11	11	11	11	11	11	11	11	11	11	11	11	11
10	10	10	10	10	10	10	10	10	10	10	10	10	10	10	10
9	9	9	9	9	9	9	9	9	9	9	9	9	9	9	9
8	8	8	8	8	8	8	8	8	8	8	8	8	8	8	8
7	7	7	7	7	7	7	7	7	7	7	7	7	7	7	7
EVANGELISM	LEADERSHIP	MERCY	ADMINISTRATION	PROPHECY	GIVING	TEACHING	PASTOR/SHEPHERD	FAITH	EXHORTATION	SERVICE	HELPS	WISDOM	KNOWLEDGE	HOSPITALITY	DISCERNMENT

What Are Spiritual Gift Descriptions?

Administration

The Gift of administration is the special attribute given by God's Spirit to members of the Body of Christ to steer God's people into effective channels of service by understanding the resources needed to accomplish goals and plans.

Luke 14:28-30	**Acts 6:1-7**
I Corinthians 12:28	**Titus 1:5**

Discernment

The Gift of discernment is the special attribute given by God's Spirit to certain members of the Body of Christ to know with confidence if individuals, teachings, or motives are from God.

Matthew 16:21-23	**Acts 5:1-11**
Acts 16:16-18	**I Corinthians 12:10**

Evangelism

The Gift of evangelism is the special attribute given by God's Spirit to members of the Body of Christ to share with non-Christians the way a person becomes a Christian and to create in those people a desire to become a Christian.

Acts 8:26-40	**Acts 21:8**
Ephesians 4:11-14	**II Timothy 4:5**

Exhortation/ Encouragement

The Gift of exhortation/encouragement is the special attribute given by God's Spirit to certain members of the Body of Christ to encourage and console the distressed and provide positive and practical steps for others to follow.

Acts 14:22	**Romans 12:8**
Hebrews 10:25	

Faith

The Gift of faith is the special attribute given by God's Spirit to members of the Body of Christ to believe God's promises and act with unwavering confidence in carrying out His will.

Acts 11:22-24	**Acts 27:21-25**
Romans 4:18-21	**I Corinthians 12:9**

Giving

The Gift of giving is the special attribute given by God's Spirit to members of the Body of Christ to give possessions and finances above a tithe to God's work with a cheerful and willing spirit.

Mark 12:41-44	**Romans 12:8**
II Corinthians 8:1-7	**II Corinthians 9:2-8**

Helps

The Gift of helps is the special attribute given by God's Spirit to certain members of the Body of Christ to help other members be more effective in using their Gift(s) within the Body.

Mark 15:40-41	**Acts 9:36**
Romans 16:1-2	**I Corinthians 12:28**

Hospitality

The Gift of hospitality is the special attribute given by God's Spirit to certain members of the Body of Christ to cheerfully provide an open house to those in need of food and lodging.

Acts 16:14-15	**Romans 12:9-13**
Romans 16:23	**I Peter 4:9**

Knowledge

The Gift of knowledge is the special attribute given by God's Spirit to certain members of the Body of Christ to acquire deep insights into God's Word and bring illumination of these insights that cannot be explained through human reason.

I Corinthians 2:14	**I Corinthians 12:8**
II Corinthians 11:6	**Colossians 2:2-3**

Leadership

The Gift of leadership is the special attribute given by God's Spirit to members of the Body of Christ to provide direction and goals to a group, and bring together resources and people that work together to accomplish those goals.

Romans 12:6-8	**I Timothy 5:17**
Hebrews 13:17	

25

What Are Spiritual Gift Descriptions?

continued

Mercy

The Gift of mercy is the special attribute given by God's Spirit to members of the Body of Christ to feel the hurt of others and genuinely express sympathy and provide comfort for those people.

Matthew 20:29-34   **Mark 9:41**
Luke 10:33-35   **Romans 12:8**

Pastor/Shepherd

The Gift of pastor/shepherd is the special attribute given by God's Spirit to members of the Body of Christ to guide, protect, nurture, and feed a group of believers into growing spiritually.

John 10:1-18   **Ephesians 4:11-14**
I Peter 5:1-4

Prophecy

The Gift of prophecy is the special attribute given by God's Spirit to members of the Body of Christ to proclaim the Word of God boldly and with confidence.

Acts 15:32   **Romans 12:6**
I Corinthians 12:10,28 **Ephesians 4:11-14**

Service

The Gift of service is the special attribute given by God's Spirit to certain members of the Body of Christ to identify, assist, and support ministries within the Body thereby allowing those ministries to effectively accomplish their desired results.

Acts 6:1-7   **Romans 12:7**
Galatians 6:2, 10

Teaching

The Gift of teaching is the special attribute given by God's Spirit to members of the Body of Christ to communicate Biblical truths in a manner through which others can learn and understand these Biblical truths.

Acts 18:24-28   **Romans 12:7**
I Corinthians 12:28   **Ephesians 4:11-14**

Wisdom

The Gift of wisdom is the special attribute given by God's Spirit to certain members of the Body of Christ to understand and discern Biblical truths and apply these truths.

Acts 6:3   **I Corinthians 12:8**
I Corinthians 2:1-13

Note: Not every Biblical passage quoted above deals directly with the Spiritual Gift listed. They help serve as examples of the Gift being used by those within Scripture or a teaching from the Scriptures.

How Does My Personality Combine with My Spiritual Gifts?

D Personalities
with the Gift of Administration

- Do not struggle with delegating
- Decisively determine what tasks need to be done
- Adeptly see the big picture and know what is needed to accomplish the goal
- Are able to work on many projects at the same time
- Have more concern about accomplishing tasks than meeting peoples' needs
- Lack warmth in guiding those involved to accomplish tasks
- Put too many responsibilities on individuals
- Demand tasks be accomplished in unreasonable time frames

D's with the Gift of administration are "get-it-done" type individuals. Their ability to be decisive and organized allows them to accomplish a great amount of work in an efficient manner. They gravitate toward opportunities where they can guide individuals and resources to accomplish goals. They enjoy working on tasks more than working directly with people. Most likely, they will not get involved with the small details, but will oversee the details of the big picture. They tend to be too task-oriented and not sensitive to the needs of people to whom they delegate responsibilities. Their lack of people skills can cause them to lose the support of those they guide over the long term. They need to be aware of the tendency to use people for accomplishing tasks.

I Personalities
with the Gift of Administration

- Use verbal skills and likeableness to get many things done
- Communicate to others how they fit into the big picture
- Understand how to motivate people to get involved
- Understand how to accomplish great things through people
- Commit to be involved in too many things
- Have difficulty taking no for an answer when seeking to recruit
- Administrate too much through people, not through well-thought-out details
- Use people to accomplish goals, leaving those individuals feeling manipulated

I's with the Gift of administration are effective in getting many people excited about getting involved. They make great recruiters, especially in the early stages of a project that needs people to accomplish goals and tasks. They are a great resource for guiding people. They are able to communicate goals in remarkable fashion and how and where each person is needed to accomplish the goals for the good of the group. Their strength of connecting with people can be their weakness in that they manipulate people to do things they do not desire to do. Also, their ability to persuade others may cause them to get people involved who later feel inadequate to accomplish the tasks they were recruited for by this persuasive personality.

C Personalities
with the Gift of Administration

- Recognize needs and know what is needed to meet those needs
- Provide accurate and concise details for accomplishing tasks
- Do not have to adjust plans because they failed to think through the details
- Are knowledgeable of the resources needed to carry out a task
- Desire too many details before implementing tasks
- Expect others to carry out their tasks perfectly
- Struggle with exciting others about the tasks they need to perform
- Bottleneck projects because of an unwillingness to delegate

C's with the Gift of administration will seek opportunities to work on task-related projects rather than people projects. They are extremely effective in working on projects where they put on paper what needs to be done for a project. While this Personality may not be able to outwardly express excitement over projects, they are extremely enthusiastic about opportunities to use their Gifts.

This person enjoys working on long-range projects. They are gifted at giving long periods of concentration to projects and not abandoning them when they do not work smoothly. They are extremely loyal and expect loyalty in return.

Sometimes their plans have to be streamlined because they put in unnecessary steps for a project. They have a tendency to make things more complicated than necessary. However, if the details are not followed, projects often have to be done over because steps were left out that should have been implemented.

S Personalities
with the Gift of Administration

- Effectively work with teams to accomplish tasks
- Create harmony among those receiving instruction
- Steadily work out the details of a plan
- Realize the balance between accomplishing tasks and caring for the people accomplishing the tasks
- Do more than their share of work because they are concerned about overextending others
- Lack the skills to inspire others to assist
- Assign tasks to others that often are not completed because they lack assertiveness in assigning tasks
- Move tasks along at too slow a pace

S's with the Gift of administration are great for putting together plans for short-term projects. Their desire to help wherever needed and their giftedness at organizing make them great at "putting out fires" for projects. They administrate through team involvement and group consensus. Their concern for people often causes them to take on more than their share of responsibility for the task to be completed because they do not want to overburden others. Their inability to decide often causes them to get bogged down and unable to make decisions to carry things forward. Also, this indecisiveness and slowness causes those they are guiding to become frustrated and feel there is a lack of direction for the group.

Personalities
with the Gift of Discernment

- Are quick, decisive, and generally correct in evaluating individuals' motives
- Boldly confront individuals whose motives are not from God
- Have little concern with the opinion of others when they realize and confront an individual who is straying from the teaching of God's Word
- Intuitively determine good from evil
- Can be unaffectionate and harsh when confronting those who have deviated from God's Word
- Determine quickly if individuals or teachings are of God without gathering all the facts
- Become angry and critical of those who do not agree with their insights regarding individuals and teachings they believe are in error

D's with the Gift of discernment are the first to detect error in teachings or individuals that have deviated from God's Word. They are good judges of the motives of others. They are bold in confronting others whom they believe have gone the wrong way. They come across as dogmatic and judgmental. They are driven to keep evil from mixing with good. While they keep doctrine pure, they need to learn how to use grace when they confront those who have gone astray. They have a difficult time forgiving those who have made mistakes.

Personalities
with the Gift of Discernment

- Influence others to recognize whether individuals or teachings are from God
- Are motivated to help others know good from evil
- Ably inspire those who are in error to turn from their error and see the truth from God's Word
- Do not use condescending words to communicate the errors they see in teachings or individuals
- Come across as proud in exercising their Gift
- Detect wrong motives in others, but their desire to be liked can cause them to refrain from exposing these motives
- Do not realize that their ability to detect error and communicate powerfully can be used to devastate others if they do not think before speaking

I's with the Gift of discernment are intuitive to discern the motives of people. Because they enjoy being with people they are often the first to detect when an individual has wrong motives. They may not confront these individuals if they sense it may damage their relationship. Their need to be liked often outweighs their need to keep others from error. Their communication skills can be an asset or a liability when confronting those who are in error. They are effective at helping groups realize they are deviating from God's Word and then motivating them to turn from their wrong ways. They look for opportunities to use their Gift to build up others who are pure in their teachings and motives more than they look for opportunities to confront those who are impure.

Personalities
with the Gift of Discernment

- Are accurate in their assessment of individuals, teachings, and motives
- Skillfully research and analyze all the facts before making a decision about individuals, organizations, or motives
- Have an uncompromising nature which keeps them from making judgments based on feelings
- Are consistent in evaluating individuals, organizations, teachings, and motives to determine if they line up with God's Word
- Can be harsh and critical in evaluating the purity of others' motives
- Look for the negative qualities in people instead of looking for their positive qualities
- Become offended when others challenge their insights into individuals

C's with the Gift of discernment are needed when evaluating whether a group should support an individual or organization. They have a unique ability to analyze information and gain insights from just the information. These unique analytical skills allow them to discern discrepancies or inconsistencies in individuals or organizations motives. They are reserved and slow to jump to conclusions. They desire to have all the information available to them before determining whether an individual, teaching, or organization is in line with God's Word. They tend to look for the errors in individuals rather than look for positive qualities. They are black and white in viewing God's Word and may not realize that while the Bible is infallible, their judgment is fallible.

Personalities
with the Gift of Discernment

- Evaluate the motives of others with reservation
- Do not look for opportunities to uncover the impure motives or teachings of others
- Desire to use their Gift to build others up and not tear them down
- Are calm and levelheaded in addressing those who have strayed from the truth
- Are fearful of offending others
- Taking needed action slowly against an individual or a teaching that is deviating from God's Word
- Can be manipulated by others into believing their motives are pure even when their giftedness tells them the individual manipulating them has impure motives

S's with the Gift of discernment are slow in evaluating the motives of others and even slower in confronting those who are veering from God's standard. They seek positive ways to use their Gift and shy away from having to use it in a negative manner. They choose their words carefully when talking to an individual or group that they discern has steered away from the truth. Their calm levelheaded way of approaching things allows them to keep others from jumping to conclusions about individuals and their motives. They believe the best about others and can be manipulated by them. Even when they discern individuals, teachings, and motives are impure, they often will not take action because they want to avoid conflict at any cost.

Personalities
with the Gift of Evangelism

- Portray confidence in sharing Christ
- Are not easily discouraged, but persistent when sharing the gospel
- Present the Gospel in a direct, straightforward manner
- Are able to logically present the Gospel and persuasively lead others to Christ
- Often feel everyone should be compelled to share the Gospel in a confrontational manner
- Can be pushy in attempting to get an individual to accept Christ
- Will often come across as offensive and demanding in presenting the Gospel
- Can come across as rude and inconsiderate when using this Gift

D Personalities with the Gift of evangelism are driven to share the Gospel. They will be more effective with individuals who are ready to accept Christ. The further someone is from being ready to accept Christ, the less effective a D Personality with the Gift of evangelism will be with them.

As an analogy: a D Personality with the Gift of evangelism would be most effective in picking fruit that is ripe, ready to be picked off the tree or vine. Trying to pick "green fruit" would most likely push someone further away from Christianity. For this reason, it is important for those with this combination to be careful (which is hard for them) with those who are not very open to Christianity.

Personalities
with the Gift of Evangelism

- Share the Gospel thoroughly
- Are effective with intellectual non-Christians
- Knowledgably use the Scriptures to lead individuals to Christ
- Willingly research questions and objections non-Christians bring up when witnessing to them
- Prone to overselling when witnessing by using too many facts
- Can come across as judgmental and critical to those to whom they are witnessing
- Underemphasize the importance of believing the claims of God by faith
- Stress the cross of Christ over the peace and joy that is available to the Christian

C Personalities with the Gift of evangelism are very effective in witnessing to those who use reason and logic to prove something is true. These Personality types with this Gift will not become irritated when a non-Christian raises honest questions or objections to the validity of the Christian message. Most C Personalities were very methodical in their own conversion to Christianity. Even those who came to Christ at an early age most likely asked many thought-provoking questions before inviting Christ into their lives.

Personalities
with the Gift of Evangelism

- Help others see the attractive side of Christianity
- Stress the benefits of becoming a Christian
- See witnessing as natural and fun
- Use animated stories when sharing Christ
- May draw attention to themselves instead of the Christ in them
- Tend to talk too much when presenting the Gospel
- Don't emphasize the cost of becoming a Christian
- Are often unaware of when to be quiet and let the Holy Spirit work

I Personalities with the Gift of evangelism are effective in sharing Christ with those who perceive the Christian life as nothing but rules and regulations. They present the joy of the Christian life in an attractive manner. They are effective in friendship evangelism by building bridges through relationships that focus on activities that are not always directly related to the Christian life. For example, they can evangelize through activities like sports, community events, clubs, and support groups.

Personalities
with the Gift of Evangelism

- Build relationships/friendships to share the Gospel
- Are sensitive to not pushing the Gospel on non-Christians who are not ready to hear it
- Do not need public recognition by the Body to effectively use this Gift
- Have patience when sharing Christ with those previously turned off by Christianity
- Allow people to monopolize and take advantage of them
- Often avoid confrontation when it may be keeping someone from accepting Christ
- When sharing Christ, may minimize man's sinfulness and overemphasize God's forgiveness to the exclusion of the need for repentance
- Often miss opportunities to spontaneously share Christ because of their caution and shyness

S Personalities with the Gift of evangelism will be most effective with those who are skeptical of Christians or may have been seriously wronged by a Christian. They will take the time to build relationships with non-Christians and will have a sense of the appropriate time to share Christ.

Personalities
— with the Gift of Encouragement

- Are driven to provide practical application for encouraging others
- Create confidence and assurance in those they encourage
- Give simple, concise, and direct steps for those in need of encouragement
- Stress action over reflection in offering encouragement
- Become impatient when others do not readily take their advice
- Offer encouragement that often is black or white, narrow, and inflexible
- Provide overly simplistic steps for overcoming situations
- Push advice on others if they believe it will be helpful

D's with the Gift of encouragement are effective with individuals who are ready to immediately take advice and implement the steps that they give. They are energized by people who take action on their encouragement. They are not as effective with those who need encouragement numerous times before they take the encourager's advice to take steps of action.

These individuals are most effective with those who are already doing something and need positive encouragement to keep on doing it. Sometimes they need to allow time for their words to catch up with the feelings of the one hearing them. People do not always respond to their encouragement with action as quickly as they expect.

Personalities
— with the Gift of Encouragement

- Encourage by helping others focus on positives rather than negatives
- Communicate encouragement both verbally and non-verbally
- Allow others to believe they can overcome challenges
- Make others believe their steps to overcoming a problem are exactly what is needed
- Aren't always realistic in giving steps to overcome a challenge
- Exaggerate their sincerity in offering support
- Too optimistic in providing steps to overcome challenges
- Provide steps to overcome without fully listening to the person

I's with the Gift of encouragement make people feel they can overcome even the gravest of challenges. They are effective in building up a person to where that person believes they are the most important person to the one offering encouragement. They create hope when others can only see despair. They can focus on others' problems while putting aside their problems. They make others see the positives in any situation no matter how grim it may be.

At times their encouragement may be insincere. Others can be disappointed when they realize this person is not as sincere as their words portrayed. Because they are so believable, they come across as sincere and genuine. They need to realize that their ability to be believed can backfire if they cannot follow through on their words with actions, if necessary. For example, they may say, "I want to be there for you and if you need me call anytime." The person calls for days and leaves messages with no return call.

Personalities
— with the Gift of Encouragement

- Give concise steps to follow in overcoming problems
- Provide encouragement with a task-oriented plan to follow
- Have great insight into what needs to be done to encourage an individual
- Are effective at listening before providing encouragement
- Struggle with verbal and non-verbal skills in communicating encouragement
- Offer steps to overcoming that may come across as critical and insensitive
- Often feel their encouragement is not needed which causes them to refrain from encouraging others

C's with the Gift of encouragement are the most accurate in determining what steps are needed for a person to overcome struggles. They give concise action steps for those needing encouragement. Their analytical skills are helpful in determining the best method to overcome the problem. While they struggle to expressively communicate their encouragement, those who know them are helped immensely when in need of encouragement.

Often they expect others to be perfect and can become critical when their encouragement is not followed precisely.

Personalities
— with the Gift of Encouragement

- Offer encouragement without being pushy
- Encourage through practical and simple-to-follow steps of action
- Are very patient with those who need encouragement, but don't always follow through on the encourager's steps
- Come across as kind and gentle when giving steps of encouragement
- May not be assertive when providing steps of action
- Tend to be shy and feel their encouragement is not wanted or needed
- Question the accuracy of their steps of encouragement

S Personalities with the Gift of encouragement are the most genuine of the Personalities when offering encouragement. They can give difficult steps for others to follow to overcome a situation, and because of their word choices, their advice does not seem harsh. Their words create peace in the individuals they encourage. Over time, they are sought by those who need encouragement. They are especially effective for those who have emotional turmoil in their lives and do not necessarily need direct steps, but kindness to help them overcome.

They want peace and harmony to come through their encouragement. Sometimes, they will not be truthful in the steps it takes to overcome a problem or challenge, because they sense that what is needed for someone to overcome a problem will be difficult for them to do and hard for them to accept.

S Personalities with the Gift of encouragement seek to provide security for those needing to overcome challenges.

Personalities
with the Gift of Faith

- Continue to pursue goals when common sense says to abandon them
- Pursue goals with a relentless and determined passion
- Do not have to have all the details before taking action
- Possess enormous amounts of courage when facing daunting circumstances
- Demand others have the same degree of faith as theirs
- Have confidence in the future which causes them to lose sight of the present
- Use others to accomplish their goals without ever seeing this flaw in themselves

D's with the Gift of faith have an awesome ability to see something that is impossible and make it possible. They are motivated in taking what appears to be foolish to others and seeing it become a reality. D Personalities are extremely suited for this Gift because failure does not deter them from losing sight of the vision. It only motivates them to work harder to see the dream fulfilled. Their confidence allows them to lead others through both action and words. This Gift/Personality combination makes them risk-takers, but often leads them to unwise actions that could be avoided if they would surround themselves with others who are less adventuresome and more conservative.

Personalities
with the Gift of Faith

- Competently determine God's promises from their own understanding of His Word
- Are analytical and calculating in determining how to act upon God's promises
- Practical and in touch with reality in determining ways to take God's promises and act upon them
- Are loyal and dependable in believing God's promises and not wavering in living them out
- Seem rigid and uncompromising in changing an action plan to fulfill God's promise to them
- Can become offended and revengeful toward those who interpret their faith as not being from God
- Require too much information before acting upon God's direction

C's with the Gift of faith are accurate in determining how to take God's promises and act upon them in practical ways. Their analytical skills allow them to sort through what comes from a human perspective and what is from God. They can devise a plan to put action to a dream that God puts upon their heart. Their perfectionist mentality does not give them flexibility in changing their course of action, even when it is apparent it needs to change. When the final results are not what they anticipated God would do, they can get very depressed and angry at both God and others.

Personalities
with the Gift of Faith

- Inspire and influence others to increase their belief in God
- People find them contagious in their ability to portray confidence in God
- Exude optimism in their attitude regarding the impossible that they see as possible
- Have faith that is action-oriented, not passive
- Can be swayed by emotions and impressions they interpret as faith
- Invent excuses as to why their vision is not fulfilled
- Are weak-willed in carrying out their faith over a long period of time

I's with the Gift of faith are great promoters of accomplishing the impossible. These individuals influence others to step out of their comfort zones and trust God to do only what He can accomplish. Their optimism causes them to move forward when others would quit before God's will was carried to completion. Their enthusiasm is often what causes others to be moved to help carry out God's will. They are able to see the positive in any situation. They must surround themselves with others who can help them live in the present. They need others to balance their over-zealous enthusiasm with reality.

Personalities
with the Gift of Faith

- Patiently wait on God to fulfill His promises
- Depend calmly and peacefully on God to carry out His will
- Live a balanced life of faith dependent on what they must do and what they depend on God doing in carrying out His will
- Are reserved and contemplative in taking action to carry out their faith
- Avoid risks when acting upon their faith
- Allow ridicule and criticism to stunt their understanding of God's will for future goals
- Prone to abandon God's direction when it causes conflict with others

S's with the Gift of faith have a tension that pulls against them between their Personality and their Gift of faith. Their Personality does not look at the future but the present, and the Gift of faith looks into the future to determine what to do today. Another tension is between having confidence in God's purposes and acting within that confidence and allowing fear to paralyze their action, which is often the case with an S Personality. When this individual allows God to control their Personality, they can achieve a healthy balance with the Gift of faith. Mistakes will be avoided because they will not take action impulsively.

Personalities
with the Gift of Giving

- Determine financial needs and decisively take steps to meet those needs
- Understand the importance of finances in accomplishing God's purposes
- Desire to influence through providing financial resources
- Demand financial resources be used appropriately
- Are highly intuitive and perceptive to where financial resources are needed
- Use resources to control and manipulate situations
- Believe giving money excludes them from giving their time

D's with the Gift of giving are the easiest to involve in providing financial resources for ministries. However, they can also be the first to bail out when the impact of their support is not what they anticipate. They enjoy giving to projects that are impacting through fresh and innovative ways, not simply maintaining the norm. While they will not be concerned with the details, they want to know that the one requesting the resources has thought through the details.

These individuals may fall into the trap of believing resources are more important than God's Spirit in the ministry for which the financial resources are intended.

They bring tremendous encouragement to ministries they come alongside and provide financial resources. The other side is they can disappoint those ministries when they pull those resources for what appear to be improper motives.

Personalities
with the Gift of Giving

- Commit their resources methodically and analytically
- Like to help ministries that are generally successful and built on sound financial principles
- Commit resources to conservative endeavors that are low - risk
- Make sure those they support are thorough in planning where money is spent
- Expect too much from ministries they support
- Are overly critical of those using their resources
- Do not try to use their giving as an opportunity to motivate others

C's with the Gift of giving are generally behind the scenes in committing resources. These individuals look for tasks to commit to that they believe are worthy. If an organization does not have sound financial practices, these individuals will not entertain any thought of supporting them. They look for well-established causes to support.

Personalities
with the Gift of Giving

- Enthusiastically provide financial resources
- Inspire and encourage others to give through their actions and words
- Spontaneously commit resources with little desire to know the details
- Are touched through their emotions to give
- Are susceptible to being conned to commit resources
- Get into financial trouble by not being responsible with their finances
- Often, do not research wise causes in which to invest

I's with the Gift of giving will inspire others to support causes. This will be accomplished through both their own giving and their words. Sometimes, their giving may be perceived as extravagant or flamboyant. They don't process information when deciding to give, but give when their emotions are touched by a need that is usually associated with people. They are often, risk-takers who exhibit a great amount of faith.

Personalities
with the Gift of Giving

- Sacrifice their own financial needs in order to help others
- Are motivated to give more to those in distress or in financial hardships
- Shy away from any form of public recognition for their contributions
- Are clear-minded and levelheaded in assessing where finances are needed
- Lack concern for financial accountability
- Are too quick to give resources instead of allowing God to teach the one in distress
- Aren't committed to providing resources on a long-term basis

S's with the Gift of giving commit their resources to short-term needs where there is an immediate result. They are drawn to those who are disadvantaged. They prefer to commit resources to people rather than projects. It will not be uncommon for these individuals to also have the Gift of mercy.

D Personalities
with the Gift of Helps

- Determine to help others behind the scenes
- Quickly offer help whether it is asked for or not
- Are prone to recruit others to help
- Intuitively determine where help is needed and respond aggressively
- Commit to working enormous amounts of time to make others shine
- Tend to be pushy in desire to provide help
- Become impatient with others who help and do not work at their same pace

D's with the Gift of helps work tirelessly behind the scenes to make others shine. A little research would reveal that many well-known people have this type person in the background accomplishing enormous amounts of work for them. Often, they need to slow down and assess where they may need help. They are action-oriented and do tasks by themselves. Because of their high energy level, they may not ask others to come alongside and help them.

I Personalities
with the Gift of Helps

- Effectively inspires others to come alongside and help
- Motivates people to look for opportunities to help others
- Spontaneously volunteers to help others without much thought
- Desire to help others on short-term projects versus long-term commitments
- Experience difficulty saying no and tries to help too many people at one time
- Are unreliable in following through in helping people for long periods of time
- Exaggerate what is required to help others when influencing others to come alongside and help

I's with the Gift of helps provide help cheerfully and enthusiastically. They receive great satisfaction in helping others look good. They are articulate at communicating to others how they can come alongside and join the team in providing help. Often, they will exaggerate the benefits of helping and minimize what is expected until the person has committed to help. They are drawn to helping people over lending help to task-oriented projects.

C Personalities
with the Gift of Helps

- Make sure the details are covered in helping others
- Provide help by carrying out tasks for others that may seem mundane
- Consistently helps others to succeed over long periods of time
- Helps others by making sure details are carried out in a precise, accurate manner
- Experience difficulty in expressing joy and excitement when given the opportunity to help others
- Feel insecure and unappreciated unless they are constantly reinforced by those they are helping
- Are intolerant of those who do not see the need to come alongside and help

C's with the Gift of helps make others shine by helping them appear organized. Rarely will those they help ever look bad because the details were not addressed. They tend to alienate others who do not agree that all the details have to be in order before helping others. Also, the perfectionist in them struggles with letting others help out of fear that something will be done inaccurately.

S Personalities
with the Gift of Helps

- Take interest in helping others often to the detriment of meeting their own needs
- Feel needed most when they are helping others
- Are highly loyal to those they help
- Have their self-esteem built up by making others successful
- Tend to let others take advantage of their willingness to help
- Need to be appreciated by those they are helping
- Desire affirmation that what they are doing is helpful

S's with the Gift of helps receive their approval by helping others and feel guilty when they are not doing something for others. They tend to sacrifice their own needs for the needs of others. They make great administrative assistants and front-line workers to those who need to personally be helped.

Personalities
with the Gift of Hospitality

- Aggressively seek opportunities to provide their home for meetings or those in need of food or lodging
- Quickly and decisively agree to volunteer their home when asked
- Determine to provide a safe environment for those in need
- Lead others in extending food and shelter to those in need
- Control people and meetings by hosting them in their own environment
- Can be insensitive to the needs of those in their family when extending hospitality to a stranger
- Are aggressive to the point of being pushy in desiring others to accept their hospitality

D's with the Gift of hospitality are quick to offer strangers or friends the use of their home for meetings or a place to live. They are determined to make their home a place where others feel comfortable. They often demand others to understand the value of opening their homes for those in need of food and shelter. These individuals view themselves as "doers of the Word" when they open their home for meetings and those in need of food and shelter. They have a tendency to be insensitive to the inconveniences it may cause other members of their family. Often, they volunteer their home without consulting with others within their home. They have a sense of control when others are in their home.

Personalities
with the Gift of Hospitality

- Are conscientious of those around them who genuinely need food and shelter
- Cautious and reserved in choosing those to whom they offer food and shelter
- Need their home to be in perfect order before inviting others into it
- Assist groups with organizing by helping with meetings or providing food and shelter
- Criticize those who do not sense the need to offer food and shelter to those less fortunate
- Are not able to communicate cheerfulness when they have the opportunity to use their Gift
- Can be too judgmental of those in need of food and shelter

C's with the Gift of hospitality are gifted at analyzing those who are in genuine need of food and shelter. Often, they will work with groups that need to organize events. They are motivated to make those attending the event feel comfortable and for the event to be a positive experience. They will generally be behind the scenes making sure all the details are carried out. They can be critical when others do not have the same desire to help others as they do. They tend to be critical of those who have needs and must strive not to analyze why those less fortunate are in need of food and shelter.

Personalities
with the Gift of Hospitality

- Are energized when people are in their home
- Create an atmosphere where those within their home feel welcome and comfortable
- Get excited when people come to their home without an invitation
- Welcome people into their home without thought of the inconveniences it can cause them personally
- Help others in need of food and lodging even when it is apparent the one in need would best be served by allowing God to teach them through financial hardship
- Use their home as a way to gain approval and acceptance from others
- Boast about their willingness to help others with food and lodging

I's with the Gift of hospitality are gifted at establishing relationships with people by inviting them into their home. Not only are they gifted, they thrive on having people in their home. They feel excited and energized when people are around them in their home. Their tender, sympathetic, and comforting Personality is compelled to welcome those in need of food and shelter. They can surround themselves in their homes with people so much of the time that they lose sight of spending time personally with God and reflecting on His involvement in their life. They can use this Gift to gain acceptance and approval from people they are trying to impress with their generosity.

Personalities
with the Gift of Hospitality

- Are sensitive to the needs of those needing food and shelter
- Create a calm, peaceful environment for those they welcome into their home
- Are slow to initiate opportunities for others to come into their home, not because of a lack of desire to welcome them, but because of their shy, reserved Personality
- Deny their own needs in order to make others feel comfortable in their home
- Slowly respond to those needing food and shelter even after they have been convinced of the need
- Are easily manipulated to offer food and shelter to others
- Feel used when others do not acknowledge their generosity and thankfulness

S's with the Gift of hospitality have a sensitive spot for those in need of food and shelter. They are drawn to these people because of their need to help others. Often, their desire does not correlate to their action because of their hesitancy to take action. They are more comfortable serving their guests than they are in entertaining them. This can be attributed to their shyness and desire to serve behind the scenes. They allow others to manipulate them because they communicate care and concern for those in need. Because they are sensitive, they often feel others do not appreciate their thoughtfulness when they provide food and shelter.

Personalities
with the Gift of Knowledge

- Are direct and decisive in bringing insight into God's Word
- Take action as a result of their insights from God's Word
- Decisively and quickly discover insights in God's Word that require action
- Lead others to discover insights into God's Word and take action on what they discover
- Are arrogant and prideful in their knowledge of God's Word
- Use their knowledge of God's Word to manipulate others
- Become impatient with those who don't grasp their illumination of God's Word

D's with the Gift of knowledge use this Gift to achieve results. They believe the insights found within God's Word move individuals to take action in achieving God's purposes here on earth. These individuals absorb information quickly and retain large amounts of what they learn. They are passionate about learning, but not just for the sake of learning. They want themselves and others to do something with the insights God reveals to them. Often, they provide their opinions to others whether they desire it or not. They demand others accept their insights. They are annoyed by those who struggle to grasp insights from God's Word as quickly they can.

Personalities
with the Gift of Knowledge

- Motivate others to desire to learn from God's Word
- Influence others to allow God's Word to give them insights
- Use their knowledge of the Bible to motivate others in a positive direction
- Have insights into God's Word that lead to taking action
- Appear to be a "know it all" that uses the Bible to back up what they believe
- Are easily distracted by something new and abandon going as deep as necessary to uncover deep insights into God's Word
- Process information aloud, and because of their ability to express their thoughts ,can lead people astray when they don't research a subject thoroughly

I's with the Gift of knowledge have insights for which they cannot explain the origin apart from God. This is unique from other Personality types with this Gift because I's do not do a lot of reflective thinking. They are quick learners who can communicate what they learn effectively and in a way that is inspiring. Often, their zeal for knowledge leads them away from their natural tendency to be around and energized by people. They have an answer for everything, are usually right, but can easily allow this to cause them to be proud and boastful.

Personalities
with the Gift of Knowledge

- Analyze truths within God's Word and explain them as they pertain to the Church
- Gather insights from the Bible and organize them in a manner that is concise and easy to understand
- Passionately gain Biblical insight, which motivates them to spend enormous time studying the Bible
- Desire to analyze and research other material and acquire insights into God's Word from this material
- Prone to desire insights into Biblical truths only for the sake of acquiring knowledge and not motivated to share it with others
- Criticize other material as they relate to their own insights of Biblical truth
- Capacity for endless analysis paralyzes them into conclusions of Biblical truth

C's with the Gift of knowledge have a great desire to study the Bible in depth. They enjoy doing word studies along with insights into the culture and times of when the Bible was written. They are adept at helping others understand these insights from the Bible. This Gift combined with this Personality type is a natural combination. Their critical thinking skills can lead to becoming overly negative of the insights others have in understanding Biblical truths, especially when they are not perfectly in line with theirs. While they are passionate about discovering deep insights into God's Word, they must constantly work to communicate them with the passion they have in discovering them.

Personalities
with the Gift of Knowledge

- Are sensitive to not use their knowledge to hurt or offend others
- Are shy and reserved in sharing their deep insights into God's Word
- Have a calm, peaceful, and slow demeanor that allows them to acquire deep insights without being swayed by emotions
- Desire to bring harmony to individuals and groups through insights gleaned from God's Word
- Prefer to specialize in learning in particular areas where they can maximize their understanding of God's Word
- Are fearful of using knowledge to offend others
- Desire to please others, which can keep them from sharing insights from God's Word that may be unpleasant to hear

S's with the Gift of knowledge are concerned with using their insights into God's Word to encourage and build others up. They are unassertive in sharing those insights, but when they do, others are amazed that they have such keen insights into God's Word. They are precise and detailed in explaining insights they discover. Because they have this Gift, their insights are often far above what others expect from Biblical truth. Their need to avoid conflicts and offending others causes them to shy away from allowing others to benefit from their insights. They need constant affirmation that their insights are helpful.

Personalities
with the Gift of Leadership

- Appear decisive in leading others
- Portray confidence in presenting direction for a group
- Create security for a group's goals and direction
- Willingly make difficult and unpopular decisions
- Demand others to follow, often without clear instruction
- Can lack the fruit of the Spirit in leading others
- Lead without a clear plan that is thought-out and well organized
- Become impatient with others who do not quickly follow their leadership

D's with the Gift of leadership most often will gravitate to leadership responsibilities that are more task-oriented than people-oriented. They are effective in mobilizing people for tasks. What they often forget is that people are just as important as projects. Often, they leave wounded people in their past. People either follow them whole-heartedly or resist their leadership passionately. You will not have a difficult time knowing that they expect others to get on board and follow.

They often work best in situations where a group has been floundering for leadership, knows this, and is craving for someone to lead them. Because of their giftedness to portray confidence for the direction of the group, they create security for those following.

Personalities
with the Gift of Leadership

- Use their great verbal skills to inspire others to follow
- Influence others to follow by creating excitement and optimism
- Develop a team atmosphere where individuals feel they are giving input to the direction of the group
- Are gifted at bringing opposing groups together to work for common goals
- Seek to lead by approval rather than following inner convictions
- Lead through impulsive decisions without knowing the facts
- Won't acknowledge and/or aren't aware when their leadership has caused harm to others

I's with the Gift of leadership make those following enjoy the experience. They gravitate to positions of leadership where they can be up front. They focus more on leading people than leading through tasks. They are great at getting people to rally around a cause. They are not as effective at leading long-term projects, but are more effective in short-term projects in which they do not have to use detailed plans. They often are best suited for situations where individuals are reluctant and/or resistant to get involved because of apathy or boredom. These leaders need to surround themselves with those who give careful attention to detail. They are great at getting projects started, but poor at finishing them. This can lead to those following being excited up front and angry and disappointed when the leader abandons the project for another project that is new and exciting.

Personalities
with the Gift of Leadership

- Accurately present the facts before asking others to follow
- Skillfully plan and present the plan to those who can follow and carry it out
- Are gifted at leading through facts and logic and do not make impulsive decisions
- Expect those under their leadership to do things in a quality manner and with attention to detail
- Criticize others when directives are not carried out perfectly
- Lead more by control than by inspiration
- Require too many facts before providing direction
- Set standards too high for those following

C's with the Gift of leadership will gather facts before making decisions to direct a group. They are often perceived as slow in making decisions, but when they do make decisions, they are usually correct and do not contain many flaws. They use facts and logic in leading. They gravitate to leadership positions that are task-related where they organize events or things rather than people. They provide leadership in what are often perceived as impassionate and uncaring ways. They may be very passionate about leading, but struggle to demonstrate this passion. They make decisions cautiously and think more about what may go wrong with bad decisions versus what good can be accomplished. They are gifted at seeing needs within a group and putting the details together to help the group meet those needs.

Personalities
with the Gift of Leadership

- Are remarkable at creating unity among those being led
- Display patience in getting others to follow
- Provide leadership more comfortably from behind the scenes, rather than in front of the group
- Portray sensitivity to the needs of the group being led
- Lack enthusiasm to get others to follow
- Willingly take on too many leadership roles and become ineffective in those roles
- Need to learn to be more assertive
- Allow loyalty to hinder making difficult decisions for the good of the group

S's with the Gift of leadership will have great harmony and unity among those who follow them. They tend to excel in small groups where they can personally touch, feel, and respond to those being led. They generally do not seek out positions of leadership, but when thrust into them are extremely effective. They can draw upon many qualities in order to be what is needed in the position of leadership.

They will lead with kindness and respect the feelings of others. The phrase "natural born leaders" most likely would not be attributed to them by first appearances. They choose to lead people over projects. They would sacrifice the good of the project over the good of people if such a decision came under their leadership realm.

D **Personalities**
with the Gift of Mercy

- Quickly respond to those who are in distress

- Exercise care and concern and take action to help those in need

- Actively seek those who are hurting and in need of compassion

- Effectively discover resources to help those in distress

- Force help on others even when it is not requested

- Push those in distress to take action instead of simply "being there" with a listening ear

- Act harshly toward those who don't share their passion for people in distress

D's with the Gift of mercy are rare, but easy to spot. They will be the first to respond to someone in distress. These individuals will often use the leadership qualities of their Personality to persuade others to help those in distress. Because they are task-oriented, they may be more comfortable working indirectly with those in need of mercy. For instance, they may give time to do action-oriented tasks in shelters for battered women or the homeless.

I **Personalities**
with the Gift of Mercy

- Others can sense their empathy and concern

- Are able to express concern for those in distress

- Inspire others to show concern for those in distress

- Possess easily affected emotions which stir them to help those in need

- Express concern for the moment, but not good on following through with their plans to help

- Can be perceived as shallow in their concern for others

- Are often too optimistic in helping those in distress

I's with the Gift of mercy are gifted at verbally and non-verbally expressing their concern for those in need. They create hope where the one in distress can only see despair. Their cheerful Personality lifts those around them. Because these individuals don't always see reality, they may create false hope with those in hurting situations. Because they are people-oriented, they will express this Gift more to individuals than causes or organizations where they cannot have direct contact with those in need.

C **Personalities**
with the Gift of Mercy

- Express comfort through their presence more than their words

- Loyally comfort those in need for long periods of time

- Accurately analyze those genuinely in need of comfort

- Self-sacrificing in helping those in distress

- Criticize those who don't share their concern for people who need comfort

- Allow others' problems to bring them down to the point of depression

- Difficulty in expressing comfort through words and feelings

The C personality with the Gift of mercy is not a common combination. When it does occur, however, this person will exercise their Gift with a few close friends. Also, it will be displayed in organizing people to help comfort those in need of mercy. This individual will be drawn toward ministries that help the less fortunate and those in immediate need. For instance, after a natural disaster, these individuals would be the first to work behind the lines to help organize both people and resources.

S **Personalities**
with the Gift of Mercy

- People with needs are drawn to them

- Sense when others are in need of comfort and compassion

- Desire to offer immediate comfort to those hurting

- Listen to needs without analyzing or judging

- Can be taken advantage of by others

- Allow emotions to sway logic in helping others

- Intervene in situations where God is teaching someone going through difficult circumstances

The S is the most common Personality to be combined with the Gift of mercy. This Personality type is naturally sensitive and concerned with the welfare of others. They are usually soft-spoken and the very words they use are gentle and not strong. Even when they deliver strong advice to others, it is not perceived as strong because their vocabulary and tone of voice is gentle and sensitive in delivering their message. When they can separate their emotions from the one in need and ask the hard questions, they make great counselors. While they are quick to respond to those in need, they also display remarkable patience with those who don't take action to get themselves out of a bad situation. They are invaluable in times of human crisis.

Personalities
with the Gift of Pastor/Shepherd

- Are driven to shepherd groups versus individuals
- Guide their flock with vision and direction
- Make decisions quickly for the group they oversee
- Protect those they shepherd with determination and tenacity
- Insensitive to the emotional needs of those they shepherd
- Are domineering and controlling in giving direction to their flock
- Become impatient in understanding others when they display shortcomings and falter

D's with the Gift of pastor/shepherd are known best for the leadership and direction they give to a group. Their strong Personality makes them ideal for guiding and protecting the flock God gives them to oversee. They are drawn to groups that lack direction and are in clear need of a shepherd. They are not discouraged by having to take over a group that has followers and few leaders. Their ability to be direct, firm, and decisive is welcomed in the beginning by the flock. Their need for control and their domineering Personality has to be tempered if they are to shepherd a group long-term. Most often, a person with this blend will desire to shepherd a group short-term before moving on to another group that is in need of a shepherd.

Personalities
with the Gift of Pastor/Shepherd

- People are drawn to their desire to nurture them
- Are motivational in inspiring those they shepherd to grow spiritually
- Effectively draw a flock together and guide them to grow together
- Have non-judgmental attitude which allows them to bring back those who have strayed
- Desire to be liked, which impedes their desire to protect those within their flock
- Can disappoint those they shepherd because of loss of interest in shepherding them over the long-term
- Lack of attention to details may guide those they shepherd along a path that is harmful

I's with the Gift of pastor/shepherd are persuasive at gathering a flock together and guiding them. They are non-judgmental and are the most effective of any Personality with those who have strayed from the flock, but desire to re-enter the fold. They are motivated to find and retrieve those who are members of a church but have not attended for a long period of time. They are interested in nurturing people but, struggle with organization once their flock becomes large and needs administration to ensure everyone is being nurtured and growing spiritually. Their need for change often causes them to abandon their flock for no apparent reason, leaving those left behind disappointed and disillusioned.

Personalities
with the Gift of Pastor/Shepherd

- Are cautious and analytical in whom they desire to lead and guide
- Are suspicious of anyone who appears to have ulterior motives in working with those under their guidance
- Systematically lead and guide their flock; know exactly where they want to lead them
- Are loyal and dependable in leading, guiding, and protecting those entrusted to their care
- Often, criticize the faults of those they are nurturing
- Desire perfectionism, which causes others to shy away from them
- Create a flock that stays "stuck" because they over analyze details

C's with the Gift of pastor/shepherd desire those they shepherd to stay close to them. Because of their nature, they shy away from risk-taking. They want those under their care to stick with the traditional way of doing things. They keep people from chasing tangents and going in a direction just because it may appear to be new and exciting. They do not show much emotion, but those whom they shepherd over time will come to covet their dependability and desire to be loyal. They are committed to their flock even when it is detrimental to their own well-being. They uphold standards for their flock to follow.

Personalities
with the Gift of Pastor/Shepherd

- Are sensitive to nurturing individuals more than groups
- Steadily and faithfully provide nurture to individuals who need guidance in growing spiritually
- Have deep and genuine concern for the emotional well-being of those they oversee
- Self-sacrificing for those they nurture and protect
- Overly protect those they guide and nurture
- Allow people to take advantage of them
- Struggle with holding their flock accountable when they stray from the group

S's with the Gift of pastor/shepherd is an ideal blend of Personality with a Spiritual Gift. Nurturing comes naturally for them. They are concerned with the welfare of people and this makes them effective in leading and guiding those under their care. Their natural instincts allow them to protect those who they are responsible for shepherding. Their unassertive Personality does not hinder them from finding individuals to shepherd because people are drawn to their desire to help others. They need to realize they can't shepherd everyone. They struggle with over-commitment in their attempt to help others.

D Personalities
with the Gift of Prophecy

- Boldly proclaim and uphold what is right
- Can be offensive in their zeal to proclaim and defend the truth
- Are straightforward and direct in exposing error
- Determine to maintain truth even in the face of being unpopular
- Decisively communicate truth when those around them are deceived
- Are inflexible in attempting to understand another's viewpoint
- Quick to label others as false teachers who don't agree with their viewpoint

D's with the Gift of prophecy are effective with other D Personalities, but often push other types away from their viewpoints because of their offensive and dogmatic stance. They view things as black and white and label others who don't agree with their views as heretical. They need to learn how to influence people by developing people and communication skills. They portray confidence, and those who desire security are drawn to them.

I Personalities
with the Gift of Prophecy

- Effectively proclaim truth in a positive way
- Inspire others to join them in proclaiming truth
- Influence others to take action in defending truth and/or exposing error
- Are able to influence others to understand truth by stirring their emotions
- Insensitive to the need to proclaim truth with gentleness and sensitivity
- Prone to speak authoritatively without proper understanding of what is being proclaimed as truth
- Use truth and great communication skills to wound others

I's with the Gift of prophecy feel compelled to uphold truth. They lead moral and social crusades and are able to get others to join them. They enjoy confrontation with those who do not uphold their assessment of truth. They feel disappointed when those on an opposing side do not engage them in debate over an issue they are defending. They are the most effective of the Personalities in inspiring others to join them in defense of truth. They also are the most effective in inspiring others to understand truth.

C Personalities
with the Gift of Prophecy

- Accurately and competently proclaim truth
- Analyze and gather facts in order to proclaim truth
- Have a strong sense of being right that compels them to be uncompromising in proclaiming truth
- Are unemotional but passionate about proclaiming truth and exposing wrong
- Come across as critical and negative when speaking the truth
- Proclaim truth with a pessimistic attitude versus being upbeat and optimistic
- Proclaim truth in a manner that is geared toward controlling and manipulating others

C's with the Gift of prophecy are able to proclaim truth in a clear, straightforward, concise manner. They are gifted at analyzing truth from error. This Personality's strong natural bent toward this Gift causes them to be passionate and often confrontational toward those who deviate from truth. Also, they do not refrain from showing their criticism for those who do not walk in truth, but deviate into false teaching. They are drawn toward those who view life as black and white with no room for gray. They often alienate those who are genuinely seeking God.

S Personalities
with the Gift of Prophecy

- Gently, but firmly, uphold and proclaim truth
- Struggle internally with desire to proclaim truth they know will offend because they do not want to create conflict and dissension
- Are patient with those who reject their proclamation of truth
- Desire to proclaim truth out of compassion rather than out of a judgmental attitude
- Often, compromise speaking what they know is truth in order to avoid offending someone
- Do not come across as confident in their proclamation of truth and in exposing wrong
- Allow error to continue far too long, ultimately exploding in a negative manner to proclaim truth

S's with the Gift of prophecy are effective because of their sincere motivation to share truth that may seem harsh, but is sprinkled with their soft use of words. Because of their desire to "follow rules" they are often the first to recognize a deviation from truth. Their reserved Personality coupled with their cautious attitude keeps them from exposing error even though they are able to recognize it. They need to be more assertive and quick to proclaim truth and expose wrong.

Personalities
with the Gift of Service

- Are driven to serve organizations or institutions that revolve around task-oriented projects
- Often serve without determining the best use of resources to help an organization accomplish its goals
- Express self-confidence in helping organizations accomplish their goals
- Use discipline in striving to serve organizations to meet their agenda
- Demand others serve the organization with the same level of intensity
- Are insensitive to the emotions of others when striving to complete tasks
- Have enormous stamina in carrying out tasks

D's with Gift of service are driven to serve by helping organizations succeed. When they serve, they accomplish tasks that previous individuals have had little success in completing. Their sheer force of will, along with a desire to serve, propel them to succeed and accomplish great things through serving. While they thrive on serving, they desire the tasks to vary and not be routine. They are driven to serve where situations change a lot, are challenging, and require a fast pace. This type individual will be able to serve in many areas and accomplish multiple tasks.

Personalities
with the Gift of Service

- Influence others to serve alongside them
- Desire to serve where there are not many rules to follow
- Inspire excitement and create a fun-serving environment
- Gravitate to areas where they can directly serve groups of people within an organization
- Don't follow through serving in one area because of new opportunities that appear more exciting
- Desire to be recognized because of their contribution in serving the organization
- Are motivated to serve in areas that have high recognition

I's with the Gift of service enjoy serving on a team where they are valued and recognized for their contribution to the team. They do not serve well in groups where there is conflict and a lack of harmony. They serve best in a relaxed atmosphere where they can serve creatively and in a spontaneous manner. This type person uses their communication skills to inspire and influence others to come alongside and serve with them.

Personalities
with the Gift of Service

- Efficiently analyze where they can best serve an organization
- Bring organization to the groups they serve
- Desire step-by-step details on what is expected as they serve
- Expect to be informed of exact roles they and those serving with them are to perform
- Have unrealistic expectations in receiving instructions from organizations they serve
- Spend too much time calculating how to serve
- Are inflexible in changing tasks or roles they perform in serving organizations
- Appear to serve with little joy

C's with the Gift of Service are drawn to work for organizations where they are allowed to serve through task-oriented projects. They are insightful about what needs to be done and volunteering to organize the details for both themselves and for others to help serve. Their ability to analyze things allows them to serve in efficient and productive ways. They often struggle with those who do not have a desire to serve. Also, they can be critical of organizations they serve because of the inefficiency of those in charge. While it may appear they have little joy in serving, this outward appearance does not reflect the inner joy and fulfillment they receive in serving.

Personalities
with the Gift of Service

- Seek opportunities to serve in a stable and secure organization
- Want expectations of their service spelled out before they will commit to serve the organization
- Serve most productively when they know the boundaries
- Like to know their contribution through serving is beneficial to those on the receiving end
- Become frustrated when what is asked of them is not consistent
- Volunteer to serve as a way to be accepted and gain approval
- Become overwhelmed when serving in too many areas

S's with the Gift of service are drawn to organizations where the environment is friendly and those they serve with are confident, but not overbearing. They are most comfortable serving behind the scenes, but can serve in the spotlight, if needed. They enjoy serving groups or organizations that have a tried and proven track record. They prefer routine, but can often lose interest in areas they serve. They are best described as firefighters.

Personalities
— with the Gift of Teaching

- Communicate with brief and specific information and facts
- Are driven to teach in a manner that calls those hearing to respond with action
- Dominate the style of communication with forceful and strong language
- Use a teaching style that comes across as opinionated and black or white
- Communicate legalistically and in a harsh and unsympathetic manner
- Are motivated to research in order to convince others of principles
- Communicate with confidence and clarity which makes those hearing desire to do what is expected of them

D's with the Gift of teaching are motivated to use their ability to teach as a way to call others to action. Generally, they are motivated to study not only because of their desire to learn, but enjoy studying because it gives them insight into principles they can use to lead people. They are able to explain truth in emphatic and easy - to - understand ways. They tend to be impatient and irritated with those who disagree with their teaching. Their forceful personality and language can cause others to desire not to listen to them. They often need to soften their words and the tone of voice in which they teach.

Personalities
— with the Gift of Teaching

- Use great human interest stories to inspire those they teach
- Exaggerate the truth
- Inspire others to change by touching their emotions with clear instructions on how change is needed
- Teach in a way that inspires groups to work together to accomplish what they've learned
- Are prone to be lengthy and wordy in communicating
- Insensitive to the power of their words to offend while teaching
- Use imagination in communicating truths and principles

I's with the Gift of teaching captivate people's attention with their colorful use of words and human interest stories. They are able to teach by appealing to the emotions of others. Their teaching inspires and motivates others to take action. They are not above exaggerating the truth and are offended when this is pointed out to them. They tend to be lengthy in getting a point across, but can get by with this because they are so effective in their communication skills. Often, they are unaware of the power of their words to impact people's actions and emotions in a negative way. They can present something as fact when in reality they have not done their research to verify this truth.

Personalities
— with the Gift of Teaching

- Enjoy researching as much as, if not more than, presenting the research
- Desire a response from those listening that is more reflective than action-based
- Teach in a factual way that may seem unemotional and lacking in practical application
- Do not teach without being thoroughly prepared with information organized in a logical manner
- Present information in a critical and often harsh-sounding tone
- Communicate such in-depth information that those hearing struggle to process all of it
- Are sensitive to criticism or questioning, especially of their accuracy of facts, or their teaching

C's with the Gift of teaching are extremely accurate and precise in their ability to teach. They would rather not teach if they cannot spend enormous amounts of time preparing their material. They may teach from a theoretical perspective, but those who are able to process the information can glean incredible insights for practical living. If they learn the skills of communication, like displaying enthusiasm, they make great teachers. Their critical thinking skills allow them to ask the questions those listening are thinking, and answer them while teaching.

Personalities
— with the Gift of Teaching

- Are sensitive to the receptivity of those they are teaching
- Present information in a calm and unexcited manner
- Communicate systematically and in practical ways
- Spend enormous amounts of time gathering information to present
- Place great importance on accuracy in communicating facts and details
- Go to extreme lengths not to offend through either presentation manner or material
- Experience difficulty in teaching truths that may seem harsh or critical

S's with the Gift of teaching desire to communicate truth in a manner that allows those hearing to slowly process the information. They are extremely effective at communicating genuine interest and concern for those they teach. While their communication style may not be flashy, it will be simple to follow and contain practical information. They have to consciously work to communicate truth when they know it may not be warmly received.

Personalities
with the Gift of Wisdom

- Are opinionated with others in applying Biblical truths to everyday living
- Apply Biblical truths in a task-and action-oriented way
- Rely on the Word of God and not opinions in counseling others
- Are intuitive and perceptive in applying Biblical truths to daily situations
- Communicate Biblical truths in a harsh and unaffectionate manner
- Demand others to understand and apply Biblical truths according to their interpretation
- Become impatient with those who struggle with grasping Biblical truths and applying them immediately

D's with the Gift of wisdom are intuitive and quick in determining how to practically apply Biblical truths. They are effective at counseling others as long as they exercise patience in allowing those they counsel to grasp Biblical truths and apply them at their own pace. They are received openly by those who are seeking wisdom and want direct answers to questions. These individuals can be so direct that they offend others who ultimately reject their practical wisdom and offensive presentation.

Personalities
with the Gift of Wisdom

- Inspire others to apply Biblical truths to everyday living
- Communicate practical Biblical truths in a manner that others readily accept
- Actively look for opportunities to influence others with practical insights from the Bible
- Focus on the positive Biblical truths in God's Word and apply them in a positive, upbeat way.
- Process Biblical truths aloud without much forethought
- Obtain insights to applying Biblical truths that often lack practical steps of action to implement them
- Lack sensitivity in realizing how their ability to communicate Biblical truths can devastate people who are not ready to receive it

I's with the Gift of wisdom are unusually gifted at communicating Biblical truths in a manner that makes others realize that their insights are from God and should be applied. They are best utilized in groups where a clear consensus is difficult to obtain. They help both sides apply truths from God's Word and take action in a direction both see as God's will. They help bring harmony to individuals and groups who need practical insights into God's truths. They need to be careful in what they communicate because of their influence and ability to sway people to their viewpoint. Also, they have a tendency to speak without gathering all the facts.

Personalities
with the Gift of Wisdom

- Cautiously and methodically apply Biblical truths to practical situations
- Deeply understand Biblical truths and their application, but have a difficult time communicating these truths
- Analytically connect Biblical truths with everyday practical applications
- Comprehend cautions from Biblical truths and give application to practical situations that keeps others from making mistakes
- Communicate Biblical truths with practical applications in an unenthusiastic manner and attitude
- Endlessly analyze every possible application of Biblical truth, which paralyzes them from taking action
- Have a passive nature, which keeps them from sharing their wealth of insight and application on Biblical truths

C's with the Gift of wisdom are extremely accurate in taking Biblical truth and analyzing how to apply it to everyday situations. They are committed to using the Word of God as the starting point for any situation that needs practical application. They like to receive and give clear instructions for applying truths to everyday living. They can be critical of those who do not use the Bible in explaining truth and how it applies to everyday living. Others often miss out on their wealth of insight because they cannot express their thoughts with enthusiasm and excitement.

Personalities
with the Gift of Wisdom

- Can take difficult truths and simplify them into practical application
- Able to put the brilliant ideas of others into practical use
- Present Biblical truths in inoffensive ways which allows others to readily accept their insights
- Have a sincere desire to help others apply Biblical truths to everyday situations
- Desire to avoid conflict which will cause them to withhold sharing Biblical truths to those who may be offended by it
- Need regular affirmation that their insights into Biblical truths are relevant and practical
- Humility and apparent lack of confidence does not allow others to glean their incredible insights into Biblical truths for everyday living

S's with the Gift of wisdom are able to take complicated problems and break them down into simple solutions that even a child could understand. This Personality's greatest strength in using this Gift is their sincere desire to help others apply Biblical truths to everyday living. They realize the need to apply Biblical truths in a patient and sensitive manner when the truths to be applied are difficult to accept. Their desire to avoid conflict often causes them to not present practical applications if they perceive others will become upset with their suggestions. Also, their need to be liked keeps them from sharing truths that will cause them to be disliked.

How Do I Understand My Abilities Profile?

Your Abilities Profile is a way of understanding the blends of your different interests and preferences as indicated by the scores on your Abilities Assessment. John Holland is credited with creating, over 70 years ago, the theory that career choices can be broken down in six areas of preferences. These six areas are: R – Realistic, I – Investigative, A – Artistic, S – Social, E – Enterprising, and C – Conventional. Holland believed that by understanding these six areas as they relate to activities, skills, and talents, a person could make career choices where they would be competent and satisfied.

The Abilities Assessment that follows is one tool in identifying the environment within which you are most effective and fulfilled. This environment can be described as the atmosphere and circumstances in which you most desire to work, and where you feel the strengths of your personality, your gifts, your skills, and your training to be best utilized. You might think of your abilities more as your ideal surroundings versus actual things or tasks you are able to do.

As you seek opportunities to serve within the church, you will be able to better evaluate several things by understanding your abilities profile. First, you will be able to evaluate the environment in which you feel the most secure in serving. This security will lead to a desire to stay involved in a ministry over a prolonged period of time. Also, you will be able to evaluate what ministry opportunities resemble your interests and the environment where you feel most comfortable working.

While you will score in each of the six ability areas, generally two or three descriptors will emerge as your preferred areas. If it is not obvious why you scored high in an ability, look back over the assessment and ask why you scored yourself as you did for each question.

INSTRUCTIONS: Every person is gifted with natural Abilities. These Abilities cause us to gravitate to tasks in our personal interest, professional careers, and ministry involvement. This assessment can help guide you in the process of identifying your Abilities.

Please follow these instructions:

Ask yourself how you feel about each one of the following statements. How true is each statement about you? Respond with the numerical rating as follows:

5 – Almost Always true

4 – Often true

3 – Sometimes true

2 – Seldom true

1 – Almost Never true

Avoid, as much as possible, a 3 (Sometimes) choice. Don't hesitate choosing 5 (Almost Always) or 1 (Almost Never). Your desire to be humble or not exaggerate may cause you to choose more moderate responses. This may affect your results. Try to be as honest as possible.

Example:

1) I prefer to work with things rather than people.

(Is this statement "Almost Always," "Often," "Sometimes," "Seldom" or "Almost Never" true about you? Try to choose the "5, 4, 2 or 1." Avoid choosing the 3 "Sometimes.")

Place your numerical rating choice in the appropriate blank before each statement provided on this and the next pages. Then, follow the instructions on the scoring sheet at the end of the assessment.

____**1.** Prefer to work with things rather than people

____**2.** Able to recognize the nature of the problem to be solved, and then find a solution

____**3.** Prefer occupations and hobbies in art, music, and/or writing, advertising, graphics, managing, etc.

____**4.** Able to socially manipulate and affect the outcome of situations

____**5.** Able to direct the behavior of others and be looked upon as the leader

____**6.** Able to teach and train by being very methodical and patient

____**7.** Usually, prefer working or doing tasks with my hands

____**8.** Enjoy formulating and developing abstract ideas that require analytical and creative reasoning

____**9.** Able to create ideas from nothing or recreate from the work of others and make it work

____**10.** Have a knack for knowing what to do and how to do it

____**11.** Capable of seeing and developing creative solutions to problems

____**12.** Prefer opportunities/tasks where accounting, computers, secretarial, and handling of data are involved

____13. Attracted to jobs or activities that are rugged, practical, and require strength

____14. Prefer working in situations that are unstructured and without lots of rules

____15. Able to communicate creatively and clearly both verbally and through written mediums

____16. Prefer to be near the center of groups and solve problems by discussing with others

____17. Often prefer sacrificing individual or personal needs for the good of the group

____18. Able to maintain high levels of concentration and proficiency in detecting needed changes

____19. Known to find my "best fit" with highly physical, mechanical sorts of tasks

____20. Most productive in tasks that require minimal guidance or direction from others

____21. Adept at using imagination along with accurate perception in problem solving

____22. Able to perceive that a situation or a task requires the involvement of others

____23. Willing to make decisions and take risks even at the expense of personal failure

____24. Prefer tasks/opportunities where dependability and accuracy is highly valued

____25. Able to keep emotions balanced and pragmatic in dealing with problems

____26. Attracted to opportunities to research complex issues and put them into understandable applications

____27. Perform best in unstructured environments where there often is validation and feedback for contributions

____28. Aware of the feeling of others, understand the behavior behind them, and respond appropriately

____29. Prefer to be in highly competitive and visible positions of leadership

____30. Prefer activities that are highly ordered and there is a well-established chain of command

____31. Personal style is usually oriented to be very predictable

____32. Able to think critically, reflectively, and with flexibility in discovering new approaches to ineffective methods

____33. Prefer to work alone or with just a few others

____34. Skilled in presenting oneself through both nonverbal (expressions) and verbal communication (good speaking skills)

____35. Able to accept authority, as well as, become one

____36. Able to work with numbers and data and organize them in a structured manner

____37. Able to understand how things work and then translate that into practical, concrete action

____38. Adept at creating systems that flow smoothly and are easy to understand and use

____39. Able to project artistic expression that encompasses attractive aesthetics and tasteful coordination of colors and patterns

____40. Able to show empathy and compassion through both words and deeds

____41. Able to merge people and projects together through effective planning, entailing knowledgeable diagnosis

____42. Prefer stable, well-controlled, conventional tasks where the rules are followed by all involved

Abilities Scoring and Graph

INSTRUCTIONS:
Record the number you chose for each of the Abilities Questions in the corresponding numbered box below. Once you have recorded the scores, you will then need to add the total for each column. Transfer the letter corresponding to your highest three scores to the space below. Usually, people are a blend of two, sometimes three abilities. However, it is okay to see yourself in just one ability. At the bottom of the chart, write the three highest scoring ability letters in the space provided entitled, "Your Code."

1	2	3	4	5	6
7	8	9	10	11	12
13	14	15	16	17	18
19	20	21	22	23	24
25	26	27	28	29	30
31	32	33	34	35	36
37	38	39	40	41	42
R	**I**	**A**	**S**	**E**	**C**
Realistic	Investigative	Artistic	Social	Enterprising	Conventional

Your Code:_____ _____ _____

INSTRUCTIONS:
Plot the totals from the Abilities Chart to the Scoring Graph below. Once you have plotted all areas, connect the dots. **Transfer your abilities code to the Finding Your PLACE profile at the back of this book.**

Abilities Scoring Graph

R	I	A	S	E	C

35						
30						
25						
20						
15						
10						
5						
0						

Abilities Descriptions

Realistic

I'm practical, active, and have good physical skills. I like to work outside and create things with my hands. I prefer to deal with things rather than ideas or people. Sometimes, I have difficulty expressing my ideas in words and in communicating my feelings to others. My political and economic ideas are fairly conventional. I would describe myself as rugged, robust, practical, and physically strong.

Investigative

I prefer to solve abstract problems and understand the physical world rather than acting upon the world. I enjoy complicated problems and intellectual challenges. I do not like structured situations, lots of rules, or working around many people. I have unconventional values and attitudes and would like to be original and creative, especially in scientific areas. I would describe myself as analytical, curious, reserved, and independent.

Artistic

I prefer unstructured situations where I can deal with problems through self-expression in an artistic medium. I prefer to work alone, or with just a few others. I have a great need for individualistic expression and I am sensitive and emotional. I would describe myself as independent, original, unconventional, and expressive.

Social

I am social, responsible, and concerned with the welfare of others. I express myself well and get along well with others. I like to be near the center of groups and prefer to solve problems by discussing them with others. I view myself as cheerful, friendly, popular, a high achiever, and a good leader.

Enterprising

I have great facility with words, which I can put to effective use in selling and leading. I enjoy persuading others to my viewpoints and am impatient with work involving precision or long periods of intellectual concentration. I see myself as energetic, enthusiastic, adventurous, self-confident, and dominant.

Conventional

I prefer highly ordered activities, do not like to be the leader, and like working in a well-established chain of command. I like to know exactly what is expected of me and feel uncomfortable when I don't know the "rules." I see myself as traditional, conventional, stable, well-controlled, and dependable.

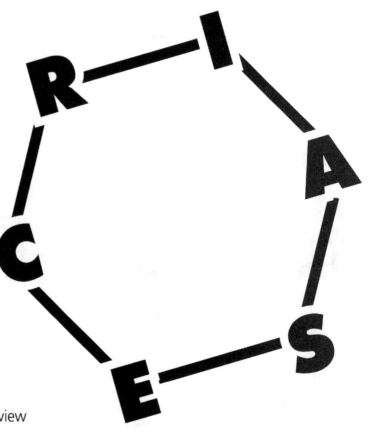

What Are Scriptural Insights Regarding Abilties?

Types of Abilities	Environments which allow:	Biblical/ Individual/ Group	Scripture References	Scriptural Insight/ Principle
Realistic	● Emotions to be pragmatic and balanced ● Political ideas to be conventional ● Physical, mechanical sorts of tasks	Levites	● Exodus 32:28 ● Exodus 32:26 ● Exodus 32:27-28	God uses physical skills in people to carry out His purposes in making a difference in the world.
Investigative	● Solving abstract problems ● Unstructured work environments ● Original and creative ideas	Twelve Spies	● Numbers 13 ● Deuteronomy 1:1-36	The majority's consensus is not always right.
Artistic	● Artistic and creative imagination ● Recreating from the work of others ● Validation and feedback	Bezalel	● Exodus 31:3-4 ● Exodus 25:10 ● Exodus 39:43	Creative expression should be encouraged in ministry.
Social	● Being near the center of groups ● Listening and facilitating	Aaron	● Exodus 32:1 ● Exodus 32:4	God used Aaron after he used his abilities in a dishonoring way. God uses in ministry repentant people!
Enterprising	● Persuasiveness ● Leadership ● Accepting authority	Moses	● Exodus 32:11 & 14 ● Exodus 32:24 ● Exodus 24:1	God puts some unlikely people in environments others would not choose for them.
Conventional	● Rules being followed ● Activities that are highly ordered ● Methodical and patient training	Aaron's Sons	● Exodus 29:19-20 ● Exodus 29:22 ● Exodus 29:38, 39, 42	There are many times in ministry where structure and rules should be observed.

Notes: _____

_____

_____

How Do I Understand
My Passion?

Passion is a word that carries intense, strong feelings. There are many ways to describe passion. Passion can be described as a burning desire for something that causes your emotions to rise where you desire it more than anything. It might be described as something that energizes you to the point that simply doing it is your reward. It could be described, if money or the opinion of others were not factors, where would you spend your time?

In understanding your passion start with knowing the source of your passion. Where does it originate? Does it come from others like your pastor, family, or friends? They may have some influence on your passion. It is from the heart that your passion is derived. Proverbs 27:19 says, "As water reflects a face, so a man's heart reflects a man." While others can influence our passion they cannot give us our passion. Passion comes from within.

While our passion comes from within there are external influences that impact our passion in huge ways. We call them experiences. Experiences will often give us our passion.

To keep from being disconnected from your passion, it will be necessary to evaluate opportunities to ensure the following passion killers are minimized:

- Guilt
- Over-commitment
- Boredom
- Incompetence

Once you understand the source of your passion, it will be important to know how you demonstrate passion and for whom you have passion to serve in making a difference for Christ here on earth. The following two exercises will be beneficial in helping narrow down how you demonstrate passion and for whom you demonstrate it.

KEY THOUGHT: To stay connected and linked to your passions it will be important to remember the words of Proverbs 4:23 – "Above all else guard your heart for it is the wellspring of life."

Demonstrate My Passion Evaluation

Check those that describe how you demonstrate passion. After checking the ones that apply, narrow them down to your top three and place them at the bottom of the page. Transfer your top three passion demonstration areas to the Finding Your PLACE Profile at the end of the booklet.

_____ **Challenging -** I am passionate about situations that require new thoughts and ideas that haven't been implemented.

_____ **Defending -** I am passionate about standing up for what is right and opposing wrong even in the face of opposition.

_____ **Delegating -** I am passionate about empowering others to complete tasks.

_____ **Developing/Creating -** I am passionate about making something that is not in existence.

_____ **Improving -** I am passionate about taking something/someone that has been created and making it/them better and more efficient.

_____ **Influencing -** I am passionate when it is apparent I have influenced others in their way of thinking and/or acting.

_____ **Leading -** I am passionate about leading a group to move into a certain direction. I enjoy determining how and what things will be done.

_____ **Managing -** I am passionate about maintaining something that is operating efficiently.

_____ **Organizing -** I am passionate about organizing resources into a systematic structure.

_____ **Perfecting -** I am passionate about doing things in an excellent manner.

_____ **Performing -** I am passionate about being in front of people with their undivided attention on me.

_____ **Pioneering -** I am passionate about launching new concepts that have not been tested and tried in any setting. I am not discouraged by failure.

_____ **Repairing -** I am passionate about fixing what is broken (this could include the lives of people).

_____ **Serving -** I am passionate about helping others succeed.

_____ **Socializing -** I am passionate about providing and planning opportunities for individuals and/or groups to get together for a common purpose.

_____ **Teaching -** I am passionate about teaching others how to understand or perform a task that they previously did not know how to understand or do.

The words that describe how I demonstrate my passion from the list above are:

_____

_____

_____

Transfer the demonstrations of your passion to the Finding Your PLACE profile in the back of the book.

People and/or Groups that I Feel the Most Passion For and Desire to Help

Check the people and/or groups you feel the most concern (passion) for and desire (motivation) to help. After checking the ones that apply narrow them down to your top three. Recognizing the list given is not comprehensive, list at the bottom of the page other people groups you have passion for. **Transfer your answers from this exercise to the Finding Your PLACE Profile sheet at the back of the booklet.**

_____ Abortion	_____ Infants
_____ Adults with Adult Children in Crisis	_____ Lonely Individuals
_____ AIDS patients	_____ Mentoring
_____ Alcoholic/Drug Addicts	_____ Ministers
_____ Believers Married to Nonbelievers	_____ Ministers' Spouses
_____ Businessmen	_____ Missionaries
_____ Businesswomen	_____ Neighbors
_____ Children	_____ New Christians
_____ Children of Ministers	_____ New Church Members
_____ Children of Single Parents	_____ Nominal-Lukewarm Christians
_____ College Students	_____ Non-Christians
_____ Couples/Engaged	_____ Outdoorsmen
_____ Couples/Median Adult	_____ Parents
_____ Couples/Senior Adult	_____ Poor
_____ Couples/Young Married	_____ Preschool Children
_____ Disabled	_____ Prisoners
_____ Disenchanted Christians	_____ Senior Adults
_____ Divorced	_____ Sexually Abused
_____ Empty Nesters	_____ Singles
_____ Ethnic Groups	_____ Stay at Home Mothers
_____ Ex-convicts	_____ Teen Mothers
_____ Families of Prisoners	_____ Terminally Ill
_____ Families of Terminally Ill	_____ Unemployed
_____ Homebound	_____ Unwed Pregnant Women
_____ Homeless	_____ Widowed
_____ Homosexuals	_____ Working Mothers
_____ Hospitalized	_____ Youth
_____ Illiterate	_____ Others:_____

Examples of Possible Reasons for People Group Passions

Some people may choose serving specific groups based on the following:

Age - A college student may choose ministry to youth based on the ability to relate with youth. This does not have to be the case. For example, a college student may choose to serve a senior adult because of a relationship with a grandparent.

Life Experiences - Someone who has lost a child may likely have a motivation to minister to those who experience this loss.

Common Experiences - A man comes to know Christ shortly after he is married. His wife is a non-Christian. Let's say his wife becomes a Christian many years after their marriage. He will very likely have a passion for men who may be in the situation he found himself in at the beginnning of his marriage.

Training - Those with specialized training for a people group may be passionate because of their training, but they do not have to be passionate for this people group. For example, an individual who works in a prison may or may not be passionate within their church for those coming out of prison.

Finding Your Place In Ministry.

REMINDER: Christians may have the same passion for certain people but demonstrate that passion in different tasks within the same ministry because of different personalities, spiritual gifts, and abilities. The other side of the coin are people with similar personalities, spiritual gifts and abilities, but their passion may be directed to an entirely different group of people.

Correlations between Personality and Passion Demonstrations

Warning! DANGER – Do not proceed without reading the following. What has been stated in the following as "likely" and "unlikely" are looking at common patterns and correlations based on consulting with individuals who have completed the PLACE curriculum. However, to assume and state these common patterns and correlations will prove true in every individual is absolutely wrong. There will be personality types that demonstrate passion in one of the areas below that are not marked (+) in the box!

The physical make-up of a human being is so complicated that not even the most brilliant scientist can entirely explain our make-up physiology. The elements we have been discussing in regard to how you think, act, do, and respond to are every bit as intricate and complicated as your physical make-up.

+ Likely − Unlikely	D	I	S	C
Challenging	+		−	
Defending		−	−	+
Delegating	+		−	
Developing/ Creating	+	+		
Improving				+
Influencing	+	+		
Leading	+			
Managing		−	+	+
Organizing				+
Perfecting	−	−		+
Performing		+	−	−
Pioneering		+	−	
Repairing	−		+	
Serving	−	−	+	−
Socializing		+	+	−
Teaching		+		

IMPORTANT NOTE: The above chart has not been statistically measured. It is based on general observations and insights. You may see correlations of personality and passion demonstrations that are not checked. That is perfectly OKAY!

APPLICATION: Take a pen and put a **+** in the boxes that correspond to the personality type and passion demonstrations if they are not already marked. Next, use a highlighter to highlight the boxes that reflect your personality and passion demonstrations. In the space provided, write some previous scenarios or experiences where you have seen your personality demonstrated through your passions. If you cannot recall any, think about possible scenarios where you could envision these two areas being demonstrated in ministry situations through you. _____

Likely Correlations between Spiritual Gifts and Passion Demonstrations

	Administration	Discernment	Evangelism	Exhortation / Encouragement	Faith	Giving	Helps	Hospitality	Knowledge	Leadership	Mercy	Pastor/ Shepherd	Prophecy	Service	Teaching	Wisdom
Challenging		X	X	X	X					X			X			
Defending		X							X		X		X		X	
Delegating										X						
Developing /Creating					X	X				X						
Improving	X		X	X		X	X					X		X	X	
Influencing		X	X	X		X			X	X		X			X	
Leading			X	X						X		X				
Managing	X						X							X		
Organizing	X											X				
Perfecting	X															
Performing															X	
Pioneering					X											
Repairing	X										X					
Serving							X	X			X	X		X		
Socializing								X				X				
Teaching									X						X	X

IMPORTANT NOTE: The above chart has not been statistically measured. It is based on general observations and insights. You may have gifts and demonstrate passion in boxes that are not checked. That is perfectly OKAY!

APPLICATION: Take a pen and put an X in the boxes that correspond to your gifts and passion demonstrations if they are not already marked. Next, use a highlighter to highlight the boxes that reflect your gifts and passions demonstrations. In the space provided, write some previous scenarios or experiences where you have seen your gifts demonstrated through your passions. If you cannot recall any, think about possible scenarios where you could envision these two areas being demonstrated in ministry situations through you.

Likely Correlations between Abilities and Passion Demonstrations

	Realistic	Investigative	Artistic	Social	Enterprising	Conventional
Challenging					X	
Defending	X	X				X
Delegating					X	
Developing /Creating	X	X	X		X	X
Improving	X	X				X
Influencing			X	X	X	
Leading				X	X	
Managing	X					X
Organizing		X				
Perfecting		X				
Performing			X	X		
Pioneering			X	X		
Repairing				X		
Serving	X					X
Socializing			X	X		
Teaching		X			X	

IMPORTANT NOTE: The above chart has not been statistically measured. It is based on general observations and insights. You may have abilities and demonstrate passion in boxes that are not checked. That is perfectly OKAY!

APPLICATION: Take a pen and put an X in the boxes that correspond to your abilities and passion demonstrations if they are not already marked. Next, use a highlighter to highlight the boxes that reflect your abilities and passions demonstrations. In the space provided, write some previous scenarios or experiences where you have seen your abilities demonstrated through your passions. If you cannot recall any, think about possible scenarios where you could envision these two areas being demonstrated in ministry situations through you.

_____

_____

How Do I Understand
My Experiences of Life?

It is amazing to watch those along the journey as they seek to find their PLACE. Many along the journey have similar personalities, spiritual gifts, abilities, and even passions. But what makes each of us so unique in Finding our PLACE are experiences. None of us have the same experiences along the road of life. It is usually those experiences that guide you into the unique PLACE of ministry God has designed you to fulfill.

The perspective we take in remembering the past molds who we are today and in the future. That goes for any experiences we have, large or small. God does not say all our experiences are good. He says He causes all experiences "to work together for good to those who love God, to those who are called according to His purpose" (Romans 8:28).

Experiences are valuable in helping us come to terms with our past. Retracing steps back in your childhood, teenage, and young adults years can bring about forgiveness, healing, wholeness and freedom. Also, experiences help you evaluate the present and future in making decisions. They can help give direction based on past successes and/or failures. Experiences can help you understand why you have been passionate about certain ministries and/or people and why they may change over time because of new experiences. It is often in understanding what God has been doing through your experiences that He prepares you for the purpose He created you for in this life (Ephesians 2:10).

Once you have come to understand your experiences there are steps you can take in making the most out of them. They are:

- Acknowledge them – be honest and objective
- Acknowledge that you survived or thrived
- Write down any lesson that you learned
- Clean up any mess and turn it into success
- Update "your story"
- Set a new goal, go after it…keep going

Successful experiences are evaluated by your determination of success, not others. Have you had an experience where you realized God had a perfect plan for your life and because of choices you made called sin you have messed up that perfect plan? Have you had an experience where you realized God the Father sent His only Son (Jesus Christ) to live on planet earth and while here He lived a perfect, sinless life? Have you had an experience where you realized Jesus Christ was crucified on a cross for the sins of mankind, buried, and rose three days later from the grave? Have you had an experience where you have repented of your sin and placed your faith in Jesus Christ as Lord and Savior? If you have had the above experience then in the eyes of God you have experienced the most successful experience you can ever have in this world. If you have had this experience, then in the eyes of God you are a success! You need to begin looking at yourself the way God does – a success.

Finding Your PLACE Through Experiences Overview

Types of Life Experiences	Insights Regarding	Biblical Example	Scripture References	Scriptural Insight
Spiritual	• Mainly happens inside of heart, mind and spirit • Personal and intimate • Must line up with Scripture • Bring about good	Samuel and Paul	• 1 Samuel 3:1-21 • Acts 9:1-18	Samuel's experience reveals it is not always immediately evident what God desires for one to do while Paul's experience with God provided quick direction.
Religious Educational	• Often allow opportunities to influence • Can provide credibilty with others • May take years before being utilized	Paul	• Acts 26:4-5 • Acts 17:16-34	Paul's religious educational upbringing allowed him to show the Jewish Christians God's plan of salvation for the Gentiles. Also, he was able to go to those of other religions and reason with them because he understood how they thought as religious individals.
Painful	• Relating to others' painful experiences is enhanced • Better able to comfort others • Difficult to see their purpose when going through	Christ	• 2 Corinthians 1:3-5 • Hebrews 2:17-18 • Hebrews 5:8	Jesus' difficult and painful experiences allowed Him to sympathize with others and showed His obedience to the Father.
Failure	• Not synonymous with defeat • Can be starting point of new beginnings • Humility can be gained through sharing failures	Peter	• Matthew 26:69-75 • Acts 2:36	Peter's experience of failure most likely was brought about by fear. He overcame his failure and it made him bolder and more confident as he proclaimed Jesus as the Son of God.
Victorious	• May be insignificant to others • Not necessarily rewarding and enjoyable • Provide motivation for future experiences	Jacob	• Genesis 32:28	Jacob's experience was not enjoyable, but had tremendous impact on an entire nation that was named after him because of his experience with God.

If you have had one of these five types of life experiences, take a moment and write down what these experiences have been and how they have shaped your life.

_____

_____

_____

_____

Experiences of Life Identification Exercise

In what Experiences have you had success, victory, or triumph? The experiences listed below are listed as examples. Reflect upon your life experiences and write them below.

_____ **B**eing asked and successfully coordinating an event.

_____ **B**udgeting finances and staying within the budget.

_____ **B**uilding an addition to your home.

_____ **B**uying a jump rope and learning how to walk through a jump rope.

_____ **C**hanging a behavior – like learning to ride a bike, ballroom dance, or an addiction (i.e. stopped smoking), etc.

_____ **H**aving someone quote you or expand on your words.

_____ **H**elping someone overcome or work through a struggle in their life.

_____ **L**earning tolerance or acceptance.

_____ **O**vercoming prejudice or bias in ....

_____ **P**romotion in your company because of leadership abilities.

_____ **P**utting others first by sacrificing.

_____ **R**ecognition in an area through serving.

_____ **T**aking over a dying group and revitalizing it.

_____ **T**rying out for a school play and getting the lead role.

_____ **V**oted the captian of your football team.

_____ **O**thers _____

_____

_____

_____

_____

_____

_____

_____

_____

_____

_____

_____

_____

_____

_____

_____

_____

_____

_____

_____

Transfer the experiences in your life that have most affected or impacted your life to the Finding Your PLACE profile in the back of the book.

Experiences of Life Personal Insights

The Bible is very clear that we are not only to be hearers and learners, but doers.   (see James 1:22)

Think back to at least two experiences that have been defining experiences in your life. Describe what it was about those experiences that impacted who you are today.

_____

_____

_____

_____

_____

_____

_____

God never said all your experiences would be good, but He did say He would use all experiences for good. These include the experiences of pain and failure, along with spiritual, religious and victorious experiences. God can and does hit some straight licks with crooked sticks.

Experiences shape our life. What types of experiences have shaped yours?

_____

_____

_____

_____

_____

_____

The process does not end with the self-discovery you have made by going through Finding Your PLACE. The Bible is very clear that we are not only to be hearers and learners, but doers (see James 1:22). The process of Finding Your PLACE has just begun. To continue the journey, you must get involved.

Finding Your Place In Ministry

PLACE Products

PLACE Personal Discovery Set $24.95

1-930856-05-9

The perfect tool for individuals who want to experience the self-discovery process on their own. Also, a great resource for those who enjoy learning during their commute to and from work. You won't miss a point. The audio series is taken directly from PLACE workshop the video series.

Set includes: Participant Workbook, PLACE Profile, and PLACE Workshop Audio Cassette/CD Series

PLACE Workshop Audio CD Series $17.95

1-930856-36-9

Great for the car and for church leaders on the go! The CD's are taken directly from PLACE workshop video series, faciliated by Jay McSwain.

Set includes: 3 PLACE Workshop Audio Cassettes or 2 CD's

PLACE Participant Set $9.95

1-930856-00-8

Everything each PLACE participant needs to complete the 5-step self-discovery process. This comprehensive set helps participants explore their unique design and understand what God's Word says about their PLACE in ministry.

Set includes: Participant Workbook and PLACE Profile

**Other products and resources may be found
at your local Christian bookstore
or on our website www.placeministries.org
or call toll-free 1-877-463-2863.**

PLACE
Finding Your Place in Ministry

Finding Your PLACE Profile

Workshop Completion Date ___/___/___

Name _____

Address _____

City: _____ State _____ Zip _____

Phone:(___) _____ E-mail _____

DOB ___/___/___ ☐ Male ☐ Female Marital Status: ☐ Single ☐ Married

Church Member Since: _____ Sunday School/Small Group _____

P

Personality Blends

Primary _____ ☐

Secondary _____ ☐

Tertiary _____ ☐
(optional)

L

Spiritual Gifts/Scores

1) _____ ☐
2) _____ ☐
3) _____ ☐
4) _____ ☐
5) _____ ☐

A

Abilities/Scores

☐ ☐

☐ ☐

☐ ☐

C

I Demonstrate Passion By:

_____
_____

I Feel Passion For...

1) _____
2) _____
3) _____

E

My Life Experiences

_____
_____
_____
_____

How to Serve

Consultant's Comments

Consultant's Comments

↑ ↓

Where to Serve

Consultant's Comments

Consultant's Comments

Consultant's Comments

Consultant Appointment

Name: _____
Phone: _____
Date/Time: _____
Location _____

My Availability for Ministry is: Days and Times: _____

Spiritual Maturity
☐ New
☐ Passive
☐ Growing
☐ Maturing
☐ Leading
☐ Mentoring

Participation Status
☐ Currently Serving/Validated
☐ Possibly Serving/Deciding
☐ PLACED
☐ Not Serving
☐ Opted out of PLACE Process

Possibility
_____
_____
_____

Minister
_____
_____

Referred Date
_____
_____

Special Events _____